BRUNCH COOKERY

by Pat Jester

ANOTHER BEST-SELLING COOKERY VOLUME FROM HPBooks®

Editor: Carlene Tejada; Senior Editor: Jon Latimer; Art Director: Don Burton; Design/Assembly: Kathy Olson; Typography: Cindy Coatsworth, Joanne Porter, Kris Spitler; Research Assistants: Karla Tillotson, Diann Peyton, Joanne Johnson, Linda Welch; Food Stylists: Mable Hoffman, Pat Jester, Diann Peyton, Karla Tillotson; Photography: George deGennaro Studios.

Published by HPBooks ®, P.O. Box 5367, Tucson, AZ 85703   602/888-2150
ISBN: 0-89586-028-7
Library of Congress Catalog Card Number, 79-54380 © 1979 Fisher Publishing, Inc.
Printed in U.S.A.

Cover Photo: Bacon & Egg Croissants, page 72.

Make A Great Morning!

The word brunch *has its origins in upperclass British society early in the 20th century. It came into common usage in the United States 20 to 30 years later and the idea has been growing in popularity ever since.*

How is brunch different from breakfast or lunch? It combines the best of both and none of the worst.

Many of us don't enjoy the first meal of the day. It comes too soon and we aren't awake enough to prepare it or appreciate it. This is not true of brunch. By the time brunch is served, everyone is awake and at their sociable best.

Brunch is usually served between the hours of 10 o'clock and 1 o'clock. It may follow church, precede a noon meeting or climax a morning of skiing or tennis.

The fact that there are no rules for brunches has endeared them to everyone who enjoys cooking and entertaining. If you don't like eggs, you don't have to serve eggs. If you prefer banana bread to muffins, or vegetable salad to fruit cup, plan your menu accordingly. And there is no required number of courses. You can start with appetizers *and* soup and end with dessert *and* cheese if you wish. The emphasis on brunch is fine food. That's what everyone will expect. And if you use the recipes in this book, that's exactly what they will get.

WHAT YOU'LL FIND IN THIS BOOK

First of all you'll find recipes—over 200 of the best recipes you've ever looked at! The recipes begin on page 23. When you can tear yourself away from the recipes and have decided not to let another week go by without having a brunch, turn to the menus on pages 7 through 22. These menus will get you started on planning your brunch. If you need help to create your own menus, look at Plan A Brunch Menu, page 6.

All through the book you'll find information which will help you become a more knowledgable and efficient cook—not to mention how this information can improve the flavor and appearance of the dishes you've been making for years. Look especially in the introductions to each group of recipes. You're sure to discover something you didn't know.

A good cook uses a variety of herbs. To many of us, herbs are still slightly mysterious. Which herb do you use and how much? How do you substitute fresh for dried? And vice versa? Information to help answer these questions is given below.

Herb Know-How

Herbs are the spice of life, so use them freely. Don't spend time fretting over what goes with what—experiment and enjoy!

If you're lucky enough to have fresh herbs, you'll need to use 2 to 3 times the amount of dried leaf herb called for in the recipe. On the other hand, to substitute ground herbs for leaf herbs, use about half the amount of leaf herb called for in the recipe. These are a few simple rules of thumb—the best judge of all, of course, is your palate.

To crush leaf herbs, use a mortar and pestle or simply rub them between your hands. Some, such as bay leaves and sage, are more difficult to crush. Commercially crushed or rubbed sage has a much fluffier texture than most ground herbs.

Pat Jester

Pat Jester understands the problems and frustrations of routine in meal preparation and the complications that can occur when you attempt to break that routine. The recipes she has chosen for this book minimize complicated techniques while presenting both traditional and innovative methods of preparing fine food. Many recipes in this book are based on the cuisines of other countries and cultures but the instructions have been adjusted to accommodate modern equipment and busy schedules. Pat is also an expert on taking new products such as mixes and prepared foods and combining them in a few easy steps to make a delicious meal.

Only someone of Pat Jester's background could approach meal preparation from so many direction. Pat is a dietitian and was a food editor for *Better Homes & Gardens* magazine. She is also the author of numerous books, including *Burger Cookery.* She heads her own company, Creative Foods Limited in West Des Moines, Iowa.

Pictured on the following pages. Clockwise from the top right: Cheddar Cheese Bread, page 83; Brandied Strawberries, page 141; French Fried Onion Quiche, page 49; Tangy Marinated Steaks, page 16; Deluxe Vinaigrette Salad, page 130.

Plan A Brunch

Because brunch is considered a special occasion, it isn't a true brunch unless some thought and care have gone into the planning and preparation. Planning a brunch menu is no different from planning any other menu. The basic guidelines remain the same. Here are few to get you started.

A well-rounded brunch should start with a beverage, such as a punch or fruit juice, and an appetizer or soup. If you want to serve appetizers, any hors d'oeuvre is appropriate. This can be followed by a light soup or by the main dish or, if you prefer, the soup can take the place of the appetizer. The main dish can vary depending on the size of your group. An egg-based dish such as a quiche, omelet or soufflé is always a brunch treat, especially if you prepare one from pages 47 to 64. If you prefer a meat, poultry or seafood main dish, you can forget about eggs. If you're expecting a crowd, you might prepare one or two egg-based dishes and another one or two meat, fish or poultry dishes. A fruit, hot vegetable or salad accompaniment is always refreshing and dieters will be especially grateful. Or you can take an entirely different approach and serve pancakes, waffles or coffeecake with assorted syrups, jams and jellies. Fruit goes especially well with pancakes or waffles. And you can still serve a casserole or two of eggs or meat or whatever you think would please.

Choose a dessert that fits in with the rest of the meal. If the meal is heavy, your guests will not enjoy a rich dessert. Keep it light and perhaps a little tart. On the other hand, if the meal has been light, they'll be eager for a rich dessert. They may even be willing to forget about calories for the occasion.

No matter what your own tastes are, have lots of hot coffee on hand. Tea or hot chocolate should also be available.

THE FOCAL POINT

The most successful menus are planned around one particular dish. That dish could be eggs, waffles, seafood or whatever has caught your fancy as you browsed through this book. Then choose other foods which will complement that dish. For example, the menu for Brunch For The Bridge Club, page 22. If you've decided Chicken Salad Véronique is going to be the main feature of the meal, a hot bread fresh from the oven and a hot green vegetable will enhance the cold salad. Minted Chocolate Mousse seems to fit naturally in this menu. It's a contrast in color and texture to the other foods. Notice that the two highlights of the meal, the salad and the mousse, are served cold and can be prepared ahead of time thereby taking the worry away from the last-minute preparations.

CONTRASTS

When planning the menu, consider the color, shapes, textures and temperatures of the foods.
- Combine a variety of colors which look attractive together. If the main dish is covered with a white cream sauce, the vegetable or fruit should be colorful. And the soup, if you choose one, should not be a white soup.
- Include harmonizing shapes such as mashed, whole and chopped foods. Don't mash everything or serve everything whole. For a small group, one mashed mixture is probably enough. The other foods should be whole or easily identified.
- Plan a variety of textures in your menu. A crisp food, a soft food, something chewy and a tender food—not necessarily in that order. Notice the difference in the textures in the Après Ski Brunch, page 10. Straw & Hay is tender-chewy with a sauce. Raclette is soft, boiled potatoes are tender, while the pickles, onions, green pepper and mushrooms are crisp. Dried beef or ham is thin but chewy. Crisp Krumkakes are filled with soft whipped cream and tender fruit.
- Think about seasonings and flavors. Avoid too many sweet items or too many tart ones. A number of highly seasoned foods will confuse your guests and they won't be sure of any flavors. One or two spicy foods is enough for one meal.
- If you find you've chosen all hot foods for your menu, drop one of them and substitute a cold food. Do the same for an all-cold menu. In the Stand-Up Appetizer Brunch, page 14, the appetizers are all served hot, but the opening beverages and the dessert are cold.

Quick & Easy Brunch

Menu

Chilled Orange-Pineapple Juice
German Pancake, below
Currant Jelly
Crisp Bacon
Brown 'n Serve Sausages
Relish Carousel
Winter Fruit Compote, page 151
Tray Of Cookies From The Bakery
Coffee

Time is precious and this meal makes the most of it. A shopping trip the day before takes care of the advance preparation. For the Relish Carousel, pick up olives, pickles and canned three-bean salad. Cherry tomatoes and lemon-dipped avocado slices give a fresh look to the relish platter. Before you shop, read through the recipes and make a shopping list. Then organize the necessary equipment and serving dishes.

First thing in the morning, prepare the Winter Fruit Compote. You'll save time by using prepared lemon pie filling. The German Pancake goes together in minutes while the bacon and sausages sizzle. Don't forget to start the coffee and you're ready for the most relaxed brunch in your cooking and entertaining experience.

German Pancake

Pop it in the oven and watch it puff!

2 eggs
1/3 cup all-purpose flour
1/3 cup milk
1/4 teaspoon salt

1 tablespoon butter or margarine
Powdered sugar
2 tablespoons sliced almonds, toasted
1/2 cup currant jelly.

Preheat oven to 450°F (230°C). In a medium bowl, beat eggs with electric mixer on high speed until frothy. Slowly add flour, beating with electric mixer on medium speed until blended. Stir in milk and salt. Melt butter or margarine in a 10-inch oven-proof skillet. Pour egg mixture into skillet. Bake 15 to 16 minutes or until pancake is browned and puffed. Remove from oven. Sprinkle with powdered sugar and almonds. Serve immediately with currant jelly. Makes 2 servings.

Merry Christmas Brunch

From the cup of good cheer to welcome your guests to the glistening Cranberry Babas, this festive menu is as pretty as it is delicious.

You can prepare most of these dishes ahead of time and keep the last-minute duties to a minimum. Both the Orange Eggnog and Shirley Temple Spritzers can be made a day ahead and refrigerated. If you prepare the superbly seasoned liver pâté and marinate the asparagus spears for the salad the day before, you can relax as you go about the rest of your preparations.

Crab Shells Imperial can be assembled early and be waiting—ready to bake—in the refrigerator. Allow 10 minutes extra baking time if the casserole is completely chilled.

Menu

Orange Eggnog, page 26
Shirley Temple Spritzers, page 27
Liver Pâté Royale, page 42
Assorted Crackers
Stuffed Mushroom Caps, page 41
Crab Shells Imperial, below
Asparagus Salad Vinaigrette, page 134
Hard Rolls or Bread Sticks
Spiced Peaches
Cranberry Babas, opposite page
Divinity
Coffee

Crab Shells Imperial

Highlight your brunch with this Italian specialty.

7 oz. conchiglioni (20 jumbo macaroni shells)	2 tablespoons snipped parsley
Boiling salted water	2 tablespoons dry white wine
2 tablespoons butter or margarine	1/2 teaspoon salt
1/4 cup finely chopped shallots or green onions	6 tablespoons butter or margarine
1 (7-oz.) can crabmeat, drained, flaked, cartilage removed	1/3 cup all-purpose flour
1 (3-oz.) can chopped mushrooms, drained	1/4 teaspoon salt
1/2 cup coarsely crushed saltine cracker crumbs	3 cups half-and-half
	3/4 cup grated Parmesan cheese
	Paprika
	Parsley sprigs

Cook pasta shells in a large pot of boiling salted water until just tender. Drain and rinse; set aside. In a medium skillet, melt 2 tablespoons butter or margarine. Add shallots. Cook over medium-high heat, stirring occasionally, until tender. Stir in crabmeat, mushrooms, cracker crumbs, snipped parsley, wine and 1/2 teaspoon salt; mix well. Preheat oven to 350°F (175°C). Stuff about 1-1/2 tablespoons filling into each shell. Place stuffed shells in an 11" x 7" baking dish. In a medium saucepan, melt remaining 6 tablespoons butter or margarine. Blend in flour and remaining 1/4 teaspoon salt. Add half-and-half. Stir constantly over medium-high heat until mixture thickens and bubbles. Pour thickened sauce over shells in baking dish. Top with Parmesan cheese and paprika. Bake uncovered 25 to 30 minutes or until heated through. Garnish with parsley sprigs. Makes 6 to 8 servings.

Cranberry Babas

Celebrate the holidays with this cheery dessert made in individual fluted tube pans.

1 (13-3/4-oz.) pkg. hot roll mix
3/4 cup warm water (110°F, 45°C)
1/3 cup sugar
6 tablespoons butter or margarine, softened

3 eggs
Cranberry Syrup, see below
Whipped cream
Fresh raspberries or orange sections

Cranberry Syrup:
1 cup sugar
1 cup cranberry juice cocktail

1/2 cup cranberry liqueur

Generously grease six 4-inch fluted tube pans; set aside. In a medium bowl, dissolve yeast from the roll mix in the warm water. Stir in sugar and butter or margarine. Stir in the flour mixture from the roll mix. Beat in eggs 1 at a time, beating well after each addition. Cover and let rise in a warm place about 1 hour or until doubled in bulk. Spoon batter-dough equally into prepared tube pans. Let rise in a warm place about 30 minutes or until almost doubled in bulk. Preheat oven to 400°F (205°C). Bake 15 to 20 minutes or until a wooden pick comes out clean. While babas are baking, prepare Cranberry Syrup. Cool babas in pans 10 minutes. Place a wire rack on a shallow baking pan. Remove babas from pans and place on rack. With the tines of a large fork, pierce babas all over. Drizzle warm Cranberry Syrup over babas a little at a time until all is absorbed. Place on serving plates. Cover and chill. To serve, fill centers of babas with whipped cream and garnish with raspberries or orange sections. Makes 6 servings.

Cranberry Syrup:
In a small saucepan, mix sugar and cranberry juice cocktail. Stir constantly over medium heat until sugar dissolves. Cool to lukewarm. Stir in cranberry liqueur. Makes about 1-1/2 cups syrup.

How To Make Cranberry Babas

1/Bake sweetened hot roll mix in miniature fluted tube pans—they come 6 to a pan like muffin cups. Remove the babas from pans and prick all over with a fork.

2/Drizzle the cranberry syrup mixture over the babas. The fork pricks help the cakes absorb the syrup. Cover and chill. Serve with whipped cream and fruit.

Welcome them back from the slopes with a cup of cheer and a lavish spread of warming food. Straw & Hay is a marvelous Italian appetizer of green and white linguine richly coated with cream and Parmesan cheese.

Raclette—melting cheese eaten with vegetables—is skier's fare and we can thank the Swiss for it. You may want to invest in a raclette machine; it melts the cheeses right at the table. However, flame-proof plates and your oven broiler do a fine job, too. Raclette is traditionally served with boiled new potatoes, but let your guests help themselves to whatever dippers they want for the melting cheese. Especially good are sour pickles and onions, fresh mushrooms, green pepper squares and dried beef or thin ham strips.

Top off the meal with delicate Krumkakes. Pass a bowl of whipped cream and a tray of fresh fruit. You'll all enjoy assembling your own desserts.

Menu

Sangria, below
Straw & Hay, page 35
Raclette, right
Tiny Boiled New Potatoes
Sour Pickles & Onions
Fresh Mushrooms
Green Pepper Squares
Thinly Sliced Dried Beef or Ham
Krumkakes, page 152
Whipped Cream & Fresh Fruit
Café à la Chocolat, page 25

It takes two hands to serve Café à la Chocolat. You have to pour the coffee mixture with one hand and the hot chocolate with the other. The two streams blend on their way to the mug and not only is the flavor outstanding, but the ritual of pouring adds elegance to the occasion.

Sangria

If you're pushed for time, make the sugar-fruit mixture the night before and refrigerate it.

3/4 cup water
1/3 cup sugar
1 lemon, thinly sliced
1 orange, thinly sliced

1 fifth or 750 ml. dry red wine (25. 6 oz.)
1/2 cup orange liqueur
Ice cubes

In a small saucepan, mix water and sugar. Stir constantly over medium heat until sugar dissolves. Add lemon slices and orange slices. Cool to room temperature. In a large pitcher, combine sugar-fruit mixture, wine and orange liqueur. Mix well. Serve in tall glasses over ice cubes. Garnish with fruit slices. Makes 5 servings.

Variation

Sangria Spritzer: Pour wine mixture halfway up tall glasses. Fill glasses with ice cubes and chilled carbonated lemon-lime beverage. Makes 10 servings.

Raclette

You can melt the cheese in your oven or broiler—instructions for both methods are below.

8 to 12 oz. Raclette, Baer-Reblochon,
   Roth, Rofumo, Fontina, Swiss or
   Port-Salut cheese
Freshly ground pepper
Freshly ground nutmeg
Paprika

Sour pickles and onions
Fresh mushrooms
Green pepper squares
Hot boiled tiny new potatoes with skins on
Thinly sliced dried beef or ham

If you have a raclette machine, follow manufacturer's directions for cooking cheese. Otherwise, cut cheese into 1/2-inch thick slices. **To bake:** Preheat oven to 375°F (190°C). Place cheese on oven-proof plates. Cheeses melt at different rates, so place each kind of cheese on a separate plate. Bake 6 to 8 minutes or until cheese melts. **To broil:** Place cheese on metal plates or steak platters. Broil at moderate temperature 3 to 4 inches from heat 1 to 3 minutes or until cheese melts. Let guests season their own cheese with pepper, nutmeg and paprika. Serve with sour pickles, onions, mushrooms, green pepper squares, potatoes and dried beef or ham. Each person scrapes off the melted layer of cheese with a fork and eats it with the vegetables and meat. Makes 2 servings.

How To Make Raclette

1/Cut cheese into 1/2-inch thick slices. Broil or bake cheese slices on metal steak platters until cheese melts.

2/Serve each guest a steak platter of melted cheese. Then everyone scoops up forkfuls of melted cheese to eat with boiled potatoes, sour pickles, dried beef, mushrooms, green peppers and cherry tomatoes.

Do-Ahead Brunch Buffet

Want to give a party with food that tastes so good your friends will call and ask for the recipes? A party so well organized that you have time to join the fun? Then plan this do-ahead buffet. It's all in knowing how to put your freezer and refrigerator to work so on the big day you'll be ready with refreshing cold soup or Bloody Mary Appetizer Molds, individual frozen soufflés, delectable muffins and irresistible Mocha Ribbon Pie with fudge sauce.

Menu

Gazpacho, page 44
or
Bloody Mary Appetizer Molds, page 39
Frozen Swiss Soufflés, below
Blue-Ribbon Blueberry Muffins, page 86
Whipped Butter
Honey
Broccoli-Cauliflower Sauté, page 138
Mocha Ribbon Pie, page 145
Brandied Coffee

When you make the muffins, try two or three of the variations listed with the recipe. Make them in miniature so everyone can have one of each. Directions for the miniature version appear with the recipe. If you prepare and partially cook the vegetables for the Broccoli-Cauliflower Sauté a day ahead, they'll be better than ever in the sauté. At serving time, heat the crisp-cooked vegetables with melted butter and they'll taste garden fresh!

Frozen Swiss Soufflés

Individual soufflés can be mixed several weeks ahead and frozen.

4 tablespoons butter or margarine	1-1/2 cups milk
1/3 cup all-purpose flour	2 cups shredded process Swiss cheese (8 oz.)
3/4 teaspoon salt	6 eggs, separated
1/8 teaspoon pepper	

In a medium saucepan, melt butter or margarine. Blend in flour, salt and pepper. Add milk. Stir constantly over medium-high heat until mixture thickens and bubbles. Remove from heat and stir in cheese until melted. In a large bowl, beat egg whites with electric mixer on high speed until stiff peaks form. In a medium bowl, beat egg yolks with electric mixer on high speed until thickened and lemon-colored, about 5 minutes. Stir cheese mixture slowly into egg yolks. Gradually pour yolk mixture over egg whites and gently fold together. Pour mixture into ten 6-ounce custard cups or soufflé cups. Cover soufflés with foil and place in a 13" x 9" baking pan and a 9-inch square baking pan. Freeze soufflés until 1-1/4 hours before serving time. Before removing soufflés from freezer, preheat oven to 300°F (150°C). Remove soufflés from freezer and pour hot water 1/2-inch deep into baking pans. Bake frozen soufflés 1-1/4 hours or until a knife inserted in center comes out clean. Serve immediately. Makes 5 or 6 servings.

Brunch For A Bunch

Menu

Double-Berry Bubblers, page 28
Flaky Cheese Triangles, page 36
Smoky Egg Casseroles, page 69
Parmesan Vegetable Marinade, below,
or
Dilled Zucchini Spears, page 133
Melba Toast
Butter
Grammy's Blueberry Pudding, page 157
Coffee

Lucky are the guests you invite to share this buffet. And you're in luck too. There's a minimum of last-minute fuss so you can take the time to join your guests without holding up the meal.

The punch base will wait on the counter until you're ready to combine it with the carbonated beverage. Crisp Flaky Cheese Triangles should be in the freezer. All you do before the brunch is pop them in the oven. If your guest list is especially large, make two Smoky Egg Casseroles. You can assemble them the night before. Either the Dilled Zucchini Spears or Parmesan Vegetable Marinade can be made ahead of time and chilled so the flavors have a chance to mingle and blend.

Grammy's Blueberry Pudding, page 13, has been a traditional dessert in my family for generations. I hope you will share it with your family too.

Parmesan Vegetable Marinade

This colorful vegetable-dressing mixture can also be tossed with lettuce.

1-1/2 cups vegetable oil
2/3 cup white wine vinegar
1/4 cup grated Parmesan cheese
1 tablespoon sugar
2 teaspoons paprika
1 teaspoon garlic salt
1 teaspoon celery salt
1 teaspoon dry mustard

3/4 teaspoon pepper
2 cups fresh cauliflowerets
1 medium zucchini, sliced 1/8 inch thick
   (about 2-1/2 cups)
1 small red onion, sliced, separated into rings
1/2 cup sliced celery
12 cherry tomatoes, halved
Lettuce leaves

In a screw-top jar, mix oil, vinegar, Parmesan cheese, sugar, paprika, garlic salt, celery salt, dry mustard and pepper; shake well. In a large bowl, mix cauliflowerets, zucchini, onion, celery and cherry tomatoes. Pour dressing over vegetables; toss gently. Cover and refrigerate 8 hours or overnight, stirring occasionally. To serve, drain vegetables, reserving dressing. Arrange lettuce leaves on a platter. Mound vegetables on lettuce-lined platter and drizzle with reserved dressing. Makes 6 to 8 servings.

Stand-Up Appetizer Brunch

This menu is fairly elaborate. Some assistance from a few early guests can be helpful, but it's not impossible to manage by yourself. So get out your warming tray and chafing dish and arrange the dining table so your guests can walk all the way around, sampling as they go.

Several days ahead, prepare and freeze Spicy Miniature Sausage Balls, Chocolate Macaroon Muffins and Banana-Nut Loaf. The day before, you can make the pastry for the quiches and Oyster Pastries Florentine. Also put together the Apricot Citrus Coolers and the base for Frosty Lime Punch. Then prepare the fruit to top the Devonshire Cheesecakes, assemble the relish tray and remove the breads from the freezer.

> ## Menu
> *Apricot Citrus Cooler, page 23*
> *Frosty Lime Punch, page 27*
> *Appetizer Ham Quiches, right*
> *Oyster Pastries Florentine, page 40*
> *Stuffed Mushroom Caps, page 41*
> *Spicy Miniature Sausage Balls, page 36*
> *Garden Relishes*
> *Chocolate Macaroon Muffins, page 85*
> *Banana-Nut Loaf, page 88*
> *Devonshire Cheesecakes, below*
> *Coffee*

On the morning of the brunch, take advantage of all the help you can get to assemble the quiches, oyster pastries and stuffed mushrooms. Bake the sausage balls, adding about 10 minutes to the recipe time if they are frozen. Arrange the baked sausage balls with pineapple, pickled mushrooms and olives in the chafing dish—remember to set out cocktail picks for spearing. Put the coffee on and warm the muffins. Just as the guests arrive, add sherbet to the punch and pour wine into the cooler. Everyone will wonder how you could be so well organized.

Devonshire Cheesecakes

Cheesecake is more sensational than ever with brown sugar and green grapes.

2 (8-oz.) pkgs. cream cheese, softened	Small bunches seedless green grapes or
3/4 cup brown sugar, firmly packed	any fresh fruit
2 eggs	Sour cream
1 teaspoon vanilla extract	Additional brown sugar

Preheat oven to 375°F (190°C). In a medium bowl, beat cream cheese, 3/4 cup brown sugar, eggs and vanilla with electric mixer on high speed until smooth. Spoon 1/3 cup filling into each of nine 1/2-cup ramekins or custard cups. Bake 20 minutes or until center is just set. Cool on rack, then chill. To serve, top each cheesecake with fresh grapes or fruit and a dollop of sour cream. Sprinkle with additional brown sugar. Makes 9 servings.

Appetizer Ham Quiches

You can make the pastry shells for these elegant appetizers the day before.

1 (2-1/4-oz.) can deviled ham
1 tablespoon seasoned breadcrumbs, page 77
2 sticks pastry mix
Water
3 oz. process Gruyére cheese, grated

3 tablespoons sliced stuffed green olives
1 egg
1/2 cup half-and-half
Dash salt
Dash pepper

Preheat oven to 400°F (205°C). In a small bowl, mix deviled ham and bread crumbs. Set aside. Prepare pastry mix with water according to package directions. On a floured board roll out pastry 1/8-inch thick. Cut in rounds to fit over the outside of 6 upside-down mini-quiche pans or muffin pan cups. Fit pastry over the outside of pans or muffin cups; trim edges. Place pans or muffin pan upside down on a baking sheet. Bake 8 to 10 minutes. Reduce oven temperature to 375°F (190°C). Cool pastry slightly. Remove shells and place on baking sheet. Carefully spoon ham mixture in bottom of shells. Top with grated cheese, then sliced olives. In a small bowl, beat egg, half-and-half, salt and pepper with a fork or whisk until combined. Pour egg mixture over olives in pastry shells. Bake 15 to 16 minutes or until knife inserted in center comes out clean. Let stand 5 minutes before serving. Makes 6 appetizer servings.

How To Make Appetizer Ham Quiches

1/Fit pastry rounds over the outside of upside-down miniature quiche pans or dishes to help keep the pastry from shrinking. Trim edges off flush with rims of pans. Bake with the pans placed upside-down on a baking sheet.

2/Cool the baked pastry shells slightly, then carefully remove the shells from the pans. Fill the shells with the ham quiche mixture and bake on a baking sheet.

Photo on pages 4 and 5.

Lazy-Day Brunch

Photo on pages 4 and 5.

Menu
Chilled Catawba Grape Juice
Smoked Almonds
Pretzels
Tangy Marinated Steaks, below
French Fried Onion Quiche, page 49
Deluxe Vinaigrette Salad, page 130
Cheddar Cheese Bread, page 83
Brandied Strawberries, page 141
Iced Tea

It's going to be a beautiful day, so invite congenial company, place comfortable chairs on the terrace and polish your outdoor grill.

For guests too hungry to wait, there'll be wedges of French Fried Onion Quiche still warm from the oven. While the salad and dessert chill in the refrigerator, you'll be free to relax on the terrace with your guests. Then cook the Tangy Marinated Steaks outdoors on the grill. If there's any Cheddar Cheese Bread leftover, toast it for breakfast the next morning. It will probably be the best toast you ever tasted!

Have large pitchers of iced tea available.

Don't rush dessert. When you're ready, take Brandied Strawberries in their individual snifters from the freezer. Garnish them with a few fresh strawberries and a drizzle of orange liqueur. Your company won't want to go home!

Tangy Marinated Steaks

Marinade not only tenderizes the steak but also adds delicious flavor.

1 cup vegetable oil
1/3 cup steak sauce
1/3 cup dry sherry
1/3 cup red wine vinegar

2 tablespoons Worcestershire sauce
4 beef eye of round steaks,
    cut 1 inch thick (2 lbs.)

In a screw-top jar, mix oil, steak sauce, sherry, vinegar and Worcestershire sauce; shake well. Place steaks in a heavy plastic bag. Place bag in an 11" x 7" baking dish. Pour marinade mixture over steaks. Tie bag closed. Marinate in the refrigerator 8 hours or overnight. Preheat broiler at moderate temperature. Drain steaks, reserving marinade. Broil 3 to 5 inches from heat 6 minutes. Baste with some of reserved marinade. Turn and cook 4 minutes or until desired, basting often with marinade, or cook outdoors on a barbecue grill. Cut in thin slices across the grain to serve. Makes 8 servings.

Menu

Tequila Sunrise, page 29
Chips & Dip
Mixed Nuts
Thermos Jug Soup, below
Sliced Roast Beef
Baked Ham
Fluffy Mustard Sauce, page 93
Sesame Seed Buns
Crunchy 24-Hour Vegetable Toss, page 140
Peanutty Granola Bars, page 151

Brunch Is A Picnic!

Spread out brunch on the beach, on the deck of the sailboat, in a nearby park or under the pine trees of your favorite mountain hideaway. This menu travels well anywhere you choose.

Crunchy 24-Hour Vegetable Toss is so good you won't wait for an outing to make it again. And it's prepared the day before. Invest in an extra-large plastic bowl with a tight lid for easy toting.

Mix up the Tequila Sunrise at home, but take along the grenadine bottle so guests can add their own. Simmer the soup briefly and pour it piping hot into a big thermos. It will taste elegant even if you use throwaway plastic cups!

Top off the day with Peanutty Granola Bars, easy to make and easy to eat. They are so good you'd better pack enough for seconds!

Thermos Jug Soup

Perfect for a picnic but so good you'll want to serve it at home too.

2 (10-3/4-oz.) cans condensed tomato soup
1 (10-1/2-oz.) can condensed onion soup
1 (10-3/4-oz.) can condensed chicken broth
4 cups water

1/2 cup dry sherry or additional water
1 tablespoon Worcestershire sauce
1 teaspoon dried basil
Dash hot pepper sauce

Place tomato soup and onion soup in blender container. Cover and blend until onions are finely chopped. In a large saucepan, combine soup mixture, chicken broth, water, sherry or additional water, Worcestershire sauce, basil and hot pepper sauce. Heat over medium-heat until boiling, stirring occasionally. Reduce heat. Simmer 15 minutes. Pour into three 1-quart thermos bottles or one 1-gallon thermos. Makes 10 cups.

Menu

Raspberry Champagne Punch, below
Curried Chicken Rounds, page 33
Asparagus Cordon Bleu Crepes, page 123
Broiled Herbed Tomatoes, page 140
Overnight Orange Toss, page 127
Buttery Croissants, right
Butter Curls
Peachy Almond Savarin, page 153
Coffee

Honor the bride-to-be and her wedding party with this elegant brunch. Raspberry Champagne Punch is perfect for offering a toast. Asparagus Cordon Bleu Crepes are delicately delicious and Peachy Almond Savarin is sweet and beautiful.

If you know you're going to be caught up in the wedding day rush, get a head start on this brunch the day before. The base for the punch benefits from chilling overnight in the refrigerator. The crepes can be assembled the day before. If you don't have time to make crepes and no volunteers come to your rescue, try the frozen crepes now available in many supermarkets. Overnight Orange Toss is another dish you can put together the night before. It's ready to toss with the distinctive yogurt dressing when you're ready to serve.

Peachy Almond Savarin is really an extra-special bread soaked with almond syrup, covered with a glistening peach glaze and served with Crème Chantilly.

Raspberry Champagne Punch

Serve this picture-pretty drink in stemmed glasses.

1 cup white Catawba grape juice
1 (10-oz.) pkg. frozen raspberries
1/4 cup raspberry brandy or kirsch

2 tablespoons lime juice
1 fifth or 750 ml. pink champagne, chilled (25.6 oz.)

In a punch bowl, mix grape juice, raspberries, brandy or kirsch and lime juice. Refrigerate 8 hours or overnight. To serve, slowly pour in champagne. Mix gently. Makes 10 to 12 servings.

Buttery Croissants

French breakfast rolls are traditionally served with butter or preserves.

1-1/4 cups milk	1/3 cup cornstarch
1/3 cup water	1 pkg. active dry yeast
2 tablespoons sugar	1/4 cup shortening
1 teaspoon salt	1 cup butter or margarine, softened
3-1/4 to 3-1/2 cups all-purpose flour	Half-and-half or milk

Grease a large bowl; set aside. In a medium saucepan, mix milk, water, sugar and salt. Heat until warm (120°F, 50°C). In a large bowl, mix 3-1/4 cups flour, cornstarch and yeast. Add warmed milk mixture and shortening to flour mixture. Mix well. Add enough additional flour to make a soft dough. Knead on a lightly floured board, 3 to 5 minutes or until smooth and elastic. Place dough in the greased bowl, turning once. Cover and let rise in a warm place 1 hour or until doubled in bulk. Punch down. On a lightly floured board, roll out dough to a 16" x 12" rectangle. Spread with 1/3 cup butter or margarine. Fold dough in thirds; roll out again to a 16" x 12" rectangle. Spread with 1/3 cup butter or margarine. Repeat folding, rolling and spreading once more. Divide dough in half. Wrap each half and refrigerate 30 minutes. On a lightly floured board, roll out half the chilled dough to a 12-inch diameter circle. Cut circle into 12 pie-shaped wedges. Roll up each wedge beginning at the wide end. Place on an ungreased baking sheet with points underneath. Curve slightly to form crescents. Repeat rolling, cutting and shaping with remaining dough. Cover and let rise in a warm place 30 minutes or until doubled in bulk. Preheat oven to 425°F (220°C). Brush rolls with half-and-half or milk. Bake 15 to 18 minutes or until golden brown. Remove from baking sheets. Serve warm. Makes 24 croissants.

How To Make Buttery Croissants

1/Roll out risen dough to a 16" x 12" rectangle. Spread with butter or margarine and fold it in thirds. Repeat rolling, spreading with butter or margarine, and folding twice more.

2/Roll out half the chilled dough to a 12-inch diameter circle. Cut the circle into 12 wedges. Roll up each wedge, starting at the wide end. Then curve slightly to make a crescent. Repeat with other half of dough.

Orange-Champagne Refreshers are classic openers for a spring brunch. Here's how to make them: Place two ice cubes in a large wine glass; pour orange juice into the glass to about 1/3 full. When the first guest arrives, add champagne to fill about 2/3 of the glass. What an elegant way to begin a brunch!

You can put together Party Scalloped Potatoes the day before and refrigerate the casserole until it's time to bake. If you put the casserole in the oven with the ham at 325°F (165°C), allow 20 to 30 minutes longer for the potatoes than the recipe calls for to make up for the lower temperature. You can also make Mom's Pound Cake the day before. When you're ready for dessert, slice the cake, top it with the season's best berries and a mound of whipped cream.

Menu
Orange-Champagne Refreshers, left
Mixed Salted Nuts
Clear Mushroom Soup, page 44
Crackers
Ham With Peach Glaze, below
Buttered Asparagus
Party Scalloped Potatoes, right
Hot Cross Buns
Butter
Jam
Mom's Pound Cake, page 154
Strawberries
Whipped Cream
Coffee

Ham With Peach Glaze

Spicy fruit glaze coats this juicy ham.

1 (4-lb.) fully cooked formed ham
1 (16-oz.) can peach slices
1 cup peach preserves
1/4 cup golden raisins

1/4 cup snipped dried apricots
3 tablespoons prepared mustard
1 tablespoon prepared horseradish

Preheat oven to 325°F (165°C). In an 11" x 7" baking dish, place ham on a roasting rack. Bake 1-1/4 hours. Drain peaches, reserving 1/2 cup syrup. Set peaches aside. In a small saucepan, mix reserved syrup, peach preserves, raisins, apricots, mustard and horseradish. Stir constantly over medium heat until heated through. Spoon some of the peach glaze over ham. Place peach slices on top of ham. Bake 15 to 30 minutes longer or until meat thermometer reaches 140°F (60°C), basting occasionally with peach glaze. Heat remaining glaze and serve separately. Makes 12 servings.

Party Scalloped Potatoes

Just the dish to go with ham or beef.

2 tablespoons butter or margarine
1/4 cup chopped onion
1/4 cup chopped green pepper
2 tablespoons all-purpose flour
1/2 teaspoon salt
1/8 teaspoon pepper
1 cup milk
1 (8-oz.) carton Neufchatel cheese dip with
 bacon and horseradish

4 cups cubed potatoes, cooked, drained
1 (4-oz.) jar pimientos, chopped
1-1/2 cups soft breadcrumbs
1 tablespoon snipped parsley
1 teaspoon sesame seeds
4 tablespoons butter or margarine, melted

Preheat oven to 375°F (190°C). In a medium skillet, melt 2 tablespoons butter or margarine. Add onion and green pepper. Cook over medium-high heat, stirring occasionally, until tender. Blend in flour, salt and pepper. Add milk. Stir constantly over medium-high heat until mixture thickens and bubbles. Stir in Neufchatel cheese dip until blended. Pour over potatoes and pimientos in an ungreased 1-1/2-quart baking dish. In a small bowl, mix breadcrumbs, parsley, sesame seeds and 4 tablespoons melted butter or margarine. Sprinkle mixture over potatoes. Bake 30 to 35 minutes or until heated through. Makes 8 servings.

How To Make Party Scalloped Potatoes

1/Combine cubed cooked potatoes and pimiento pieces in a baking dish. Pour in the horseradish-flavored cream sauce and mix gently.

2/To make the crumb topping, mix the melted butter or margarine, breadcrumbs, sesame seeds and snipped parsley in a small bowl. Sprinkle the topping over the casserole and bake until bubbly.

Brunch For The Bridge Club

Get an early start at the bridge table by inviting your friends for a late brunch. Chicken Salad Véronique has a delicious mayonnaise and yogurt dressing subtly flavored with white wine and mustard. Make the frosted grapes ahead so the lime-gelatin coating will have time to dry completely. A small slice of melon is another attractive garnish for this salad.

If you have time, make Bubble Bread and serve it warm. If time is an important factor, stir up the popovers. Both breads are unique, so whichever you choose, you'll impress your guests.

They haven't tasted anything until you bring out dessert! Spoon the light and delicate Minted Chocolate Mousse into your prettiest sherbet dishes early in the morning—or even the night before—and chill them until serving time. Then top each mousse with a peak of whipped cream and a garnish of chocolate curls. Fantastic!

Menu

Chicken Salad Véronique, page 105
Herbal Popovers, page 86
or
Bubble Bread, page 85
Hot Buttered Peas
Minted Chocolate Mousse, below
Iced Tea

Minted Chocolate Mousse

Use a swivel-bladed vegetable peeler to shave curls from chocolate squares.

1 (6-oz.) pkg. semisweet chocolate pieces
1/4 cup chocolate mint liqueur
6 eggs, separated

1-1/2 teaspoons vanilla extract
2 cups whipping cream
Chocolate curls

In the top of a double boiler, mix chocolate pieces and liqueur. Stir occasionally over simmering water until chocolate melts. In a small bowl, beat egg whites with electric mixer on high speed until stiff peaks form; set aside. In another small bowl, beat egg yolks with electric mixer on high speed until thickened and lemon-colored, about 5 minutes. Stir a small amount of melted chocolate into egg yolks; return to chocolate in double boiler. Beat well. Stir in vanilla. Cool. In another small bowl, beat whipping cream with electric mixer on high speed until soft peaks form. Reserve about 1 cup whipped cream for garnish. Cover and refrigerate. Fold remaining whipped cream and egg whites into chocolate mixture. Spoon into a 1-quart serving dish or 8 individual dishes. Chill until firm, 3 to 4 hours. Garnish with reserved whipped cream and chocolate curls. Makes 8 servings.

Beverages

The cup that cheers, with or without spirits, is a delightful way to begin brunch. Depending on your guests, you may decide to offer one beverage with spirits and a second without.

In general, serve chilled beverages before the food and hot drinks, like coffee, tea or chocolate at the end of the meal.

Wine is a basic ingredient for many of the punches. Buy good jug wine for these recipes. The punch covers up any differences between fine wine and good inexpensive wine, so save your finer wine for dinner. Most of these recipes are open to variation. You can increase or decrease the proportions according to your taste.

Many of the beverages in this section can be mixed the day before to blend the flavors. Others are easy and quick enough to mix just before the party. Or set out the ingredients and let the guests stir up their own.

Chocolate Potion, which is the base for Magic Hot Chocolate, is a sweetened, thickened chocolate concentrate. The recipe calls for adding hot milk to the concentrate, but one guest who dislikes milk asked for hot water and went home with the recipe in her hand. This same chocolate concentrate has been served over ice cream and even spread on slices of cake. Whether you add hot milk or hot water or use it as a topping, the flavor is heavenly!

Shirley Temple Spritzers and Frosty Lime Punch are popular with the younger set.

If you're looking for a Sangria recipe, it's with the menus on page 10 and Orange-Champagne Refreshers are on page 20.

Collect some attractive serving gear such as an ice bucket, an insulated pitcher or air pot, delicate stemmed glasses, handsome mugs, a pretty punch bowl and cups. You'll find a warming tray is a boon for keeping hot beverages at the right temperature.

Apricot Citrus Coolers

Mix the syrup the night before and all you have to do in the morning is add ice cubes and wine.

1 orange
1 lemon
1 cup apricot nectar
1/4 cup apricot preserves
2 tablespoons powdered sugar

6 inches stick cinnamon
Ice cubes
2 fifths or 1.5 liters Chablis wine (51.2 oz.)
Orange and lemon slices

Peel orange and lemon. Cut peels into slivers. Squeeze juice from orange and lemon. In a medium saucepan, mix orange peel slivers, lemon peel slivers, orange juice, lemon juice, apricot nectar, apricot preserves, powdered sugar and cinnamon sticks. Bring to a boil. Reduce heat and simmer 10 minutes. Chill. At serving time, strain mixture into a large pitcher. Add ice cubes and wine. Stir to mix. Serve in wine glasses garnished with orange and lemon slices. Makes 12 to 16 servings.

Café à la Chocolat

Here's a chance to pour from your prettiest coffee and chocolate servers.

Ground coffee (drip or percolator grind)
1 whole nutmeg
3 inches stick cinnamon
6 cups water

4 cups milk
4 (1-oz.) squares semisweet chocolate, cut up
1/3 cup sugar
1 teaspoon vanilla extract

Place enough ground coffee in the basket of a percolator or drip coffeemaker to yield 8 cups of strong coffee. Add whole nutmeg and stick cinnamon to ground coffee. Pour 6 measuring cups water into the percolator or coffeemaker and brew coffee according to manufacturer's directions. In a heavy saucepan, mix milk, chocolate and sugar. Stir constantly over medium heat until chocolate just melts. Stir in vanilla. To serve, *at the same time*, pour hot coffee and hot chocolate milk mixture into serving cups. Makes 8 to 10 servings.

Variation

Spirited Café à la Chocolat: Decrease sugar to 2 tablespoons. Pour 1 jigger (1-1/2 ounces) coffee-flavored liqueur or crème de cacao into each cup before pouring in hot coffee and chocolate mixture.

Magic Hot Chocolate

Chocolate Potion will keep in the refrigerator up to one week.

Chocolate Potion, see below
6 cups hot milk

Chocolate Potion:
1 (15-oz.) can sweetened condensed milk
1 (4-oz.) bar German sweet cooking
   chocolate, broken in pieces

1 cup whipping cream, whipped

Spoon 1/4 cup Chocolate Potion into each of 12 mugs. Add 1/2 cup hot milk to each mug. Stir until blended. Makes 12 servings.

Chocolate Potion:

In a small saucepan, mix condensed milk and chocolate pieces. Stir constantly over low heat until chocolate melts. Cool to room temperature. Fold in whipped cream. Use immediately or cover and store in refrigerator.

If you are using glass mugs for hot drinks, pour the drink into the mug over the back of a metal spoon to avoid cracking the mugs.

Café à la Chocolat

Hot Cocomocha

You'll like this after-brunch coffee!

3/4 cup coffee-flavored liqueur
1/4 cup crème de cacao
1/4 cup orange-flavored liqueur
1/4 cup brandy

6 cups hot strong coffee
1 (4-1/2-oz.) carton frozen whipped
   dessert topping, thawed
Orange Twists, page 147

In a 2-cup measure, mix coffee liqueur, crème de cacao, orange-flavored liqueur and brandy. To serve, add 3 tablespoons of the liqueur mixture to each of 8 mugs. Pour coffee to within 1 inch of top of each mug; mix well. Top with whipped topping and garnish with orange twists. Makes 8 servings.

Orange Eggnog

It's the familiar holiday favorite with a citrus flavor.

1 qt. canned or dairy eggnog
1-1/2 cups milk
1 (6-oz.) can frozen orange juice concentrate,
   thawed
1/2 cup light rum

1/4 cup orange-flavored liqueur
Whipped topping
Ground nutmeg
Orange slices, if desired

In a large pitcher, mix eggnog, milk, orange juice concentrate, rum and orange liqueur. Refrigerate several hours or overnight to blend flavors. To serve, pour into small mugs. Top with whipped topping and sprinkle with nutmeg. Garnish with orange slices if desired. Makes 8 servings.

Spiced Orange Tea

Orange juice and just-right spicing do wonderful things for a cup of tea.

4 cups water
2 cups orange juice
1/2 cup honey
3 inches stick cinnamon

4 teaspoons loose tea or 4 tea bags
1 orange, unpeeled, cut in 8 wedges
16 whole cloves

In a large saucepan, mix water, orange juice, honey and cinnamon. Bring to a boil. Reduce heat, cover and simmer 15 minutes. Bring again to a full boil. Remove from heat. Add loose tea or tea bags; let steep 3 to 5 minutes. Discard cinnamon stick. Stud 6 or 7 orange wedges with cloves. Place 1 orange wedge in each of 6 or 7 mugs. Pour hot tea into mugs. Makes 6 or 7 servings.

Tropical Tangerine Coolers

Great combination of flavors here. Frozen lemon yogurt adds a pleasant tang.

1 (3-oz.) pkg. lemon-flavored gelatin
1 cup boiling water
1 (6-oz.) can frozen tangerine juice
   concentrate, thawed

3 cups cold water
1 qt. lemon frozen yogurt
1 (28-oz.) bottle ginger ale, chilled
Tangerine slices

In a large bowl, dissolve gelatin in boiling water. Stir in tangerine juice concentrate. Add cold water. Refrigerate until serving time. To serve, place a scoop of lemon frozen yogurt in each of 8 tall glasses. Pour tangerine mixture halfway up each glass. Pour ginger ale down side of each glass to fill. Garnish with tangerine slices. Makes 8 servings.

Frosty Lime Punch

Something special in the beverage line. Pretty and delicious!

1 (6-oz.) can frozen limeade concentrate,
   thawed
1 (6-oz.) can frozen lemonade concentrate,
   thawed
6 cups cold water
1/4 cup lemon juice

1 pint lime sherbet
2 (33-oz.) bottles lemon-lime carbonated
   beverage, chilled
Lemon slices
Lime slices
Mint leaves

In a punch bowl, mix limeade concentrate, lemonade concentrate, cold water and lemon juice. Chill. At serving time, spoon sherbet into punch bowl. Carefully pour carbonated beverage down side of bowl. Mix gently. Garnish with lemon and lime slices and mint leaves. Makes about 20 servings.

Shirley Temple Spritzers

Tastes as good as it looks.

1 (14-oz.) jar spiced apple rings
   in heavy syrup
2 cups apple juice
1 (6-oz.) can frozen lemonade concentrate,
   thawed

1 lemon, thinly sliced
Ice cubes
1 fifth or 750 ml. sparkling Catawba
   grape juice, chilled (25.6 oz.)

Drain syrup from apple slices into a large pitcher. Refrigerate apple slices. Add apple juice, lemonade concentrate and lemon slices to syrup; mix well. Refrigerate 8 hours or overnight. To serve, add ice cubes to pitcher. Slowly pour in sparkling Catawba grape juice. Serve in tall glasses. Garnish with apple rings and lemon slices. Makes 6 servings.

Peach Melba Fizz

Substitute ginger ale for the champagne if you want a non-alcoholic beverage.

2 large fresh peaches, peeled,
  halved, pitted

1 pint raspberry sherbet
2 cups pink champagne, chilled

Place a peach half in each of 4 champagne glasses. Top each peach half with a generous scoop of raspberry sherbet. Pour 1/2 cup pink champagne into each glass. Makes 4 servings.

Variation

Strawberry Fizzes: Substitute 1 pint fresh strawberries, hulled and halved, for the peaches. Substitute 1 pint strawberry ice cream for the raspberry sherbet.

Double-Berry Bubblers

This refreshing punch will be especially popular in the summer.

3 cups cranberry juice cocktail
1 (3-oz.) pkg. strawberry-flavored gelatin
1 cup fresh or thawed frozen strawberries
2 tablespoons lemon juice

Ice cubes
3 (12-oz.) cans strawberry carbonated
  beverage, chilled
Fresh strawberries, if desired

In a medium saucepan, bring 1 cup cranberry juice cocktail to a boil. Stir in gelatin until dissolved. Stir in remaining cranberry juice, 1 cup strawberries and lemon juice. Remove from heat and cool to room temperature. To serve, place ice cubes in tall glasses. Pour cranberry mixture halfway up each glass. Fill glasses with strawberry carbonated beverage. Stir to just mix. Garnish with strawberries, if desired. Makes 8 servings.

Sparkling Pineapple Refresher

Switch strawberries for grapes for a different look.

2 cups Rhine wine
1/2 cup pineapple juice
2 tablespoons powdered sugar
1 cup cubed fresh pineapple

1/2 cup red grapes
1 fifth or 750 ml. sparkling rosé wine
  (25.6 oz.), chilled

In a large pitcher, mix Rhine wine, pineapple juice and powdered sugar. Stir to dissolve sugar. Add pineapple cubes and grapes. Chill. At serving time, slowly pour sparkling rosé into pitcher. Mix gently. Makes 6 servings.

Tequila Sunrise

Determine the sweetness of this Mexican classic by the amount of grenadine you use.

Ice cubes
1 jigger tequila (1-1/2-oz.)
1/2 cup orange juice
2 teaspoons lime juice

1 to 2 tablespoons grenadine
Orange Twist, page 147
Maraschino cherry

Place ice cubes in a tall glass. Add tequila, orange juice and lime juice. Stir to just mix. Slowly add grenadine. Do not stir. Garnish with an Orange Twist and maraschino cherry. Makes 1 serving.

Pousse Café à la Juice

Layer fruit juices instead of liqueurs. And it's pronounced poose kafay.

2 cups cranberry-apple juice, chilled
2 cups papaya or apricot nectar, chilled

Apple slices
Fresh cranberries

Chill six 6-ounce tall narrow glasses. In each chilled glass, pour 1/3 cup cranberry-apple juice. Tilt each glass and slowly pour 1/3 cup nectar down the side. Garnish with an apple slice and cranberries . Serve at once. Makes 6 servings.

How To Make Pousse Café à la Juice

1/Pour 1/3 cup cranberry-apple juice into a chilled narrow glass, carefully pour 1/3 cup papaya or apricot nectar down the side of the glass to form a layer on top of juice.

2/Use a wooden pick to skewer fresh cranberries and apple slices. Place skewered fruit across glass rims to garnish. Serve immediately before the layers begin to blend.

Harvey Wallbanger Slush

The solution to the last minute rush—this one waits in the freezer.

5 cups orange juice
3/4 cup vodka
1/3 cup Galliano liqueur

Orange slices
Maraschino cherries

In a large bowl, mix orange juice, vodka and Galliano. Stir to mix well. Pour into a 2-quart freezer container. Freeze 6 hours or overnight until slushy; mixture will not freeze firm. To serve, spoon into stemmed glasses and garnish with an orange slice and maraschino cherry. Makes 6 servings.

Screwdrivers

Have extra ingredients on hand—guests always ask for seconds.

1 (12-oz.) can frozen orange juice
  concentrate, thawed
Water
1-1/2 cups vodka

1 to 2 teaspoons powdered sugar, if desired
Ice cubes
Orange slices
Maraschino cherries

In a large pitcher, mix orange juice concentrate and 3 juice cans of water. Stir in vodka. Add powdered sugar to taste, if desired. Refrigerate until serving time. Serve in tall glasses over ice cubes. Garnish with orange slices and maraschino cherries. Makes 8 servings.

Variation

Orange Blossoms: Substitute gin for vodka.

Ramos Fizz

Tart and tantalizing!

4 jiggers gin (6 oz.)
4 egg whites
1/4 cup powdered sugar
1/4 cup whipping cream
1/4 cup lime juice
2 tablespoons pineapple juice

1/4 teaspoon vanilla extract
1 drop orange extract
2 cups crushed ice
Lime juice
Granulated sugar

In blender container, mix gin, egg whites, powdered sugar, cream, 1/4 cup lime juice, pineapple juice, vanilla, orange extract and crushed ice. Cover and process with blender on high speed until frothy. Dip the rims of 4 stemmed glasses in lime juice, then in granulated sugar. Pour fizzes into prepared glasses. Makes 4 servings.

Fresh Peach-Cherry Spritzers

Look for ascorbic acid color keeper in the canning section of your supermarket.

2 fresh peaches, peeled, sliced
6 to 8 fresh sweet cherries with stems
1/2 cup cherry brandy
1/4 cup peach brandy

2 teaspoons ascorbic acid color keeper
1 fifth or 750 ml. Moselle wine
   (25.6 oz.), chilled
2 cups carbonated soda water, chilled

In a large pitcher, mix peaches, cherries, cherry brandy, peach brandy and ascorbic acid color keeper. Refrigerate 8 hours or overnight. Chill 6 to 8 stemmed glasses. At serving time, add wine and carbonated soda water to mixture in pitcher. Mix gently. Serve in chilled glasses, garnished with peach slices and cherries. Makes 6 to 8 servings.

How To Make Fresh Peach-Cherry Spritzers

1/In a glass pitcher, marinate peach slices and cherries in cherry and peach brandy. Ascorbic acid color keeper helps keep the peaches from darkening while they are marinating.

2/After marinating the fruits, pour chilled Moselle wine into the pitcher. Just before serving, slowly add carbonated water to the fruit-wine mixture to retain as much fizz as possible. Mix gently and serve in punch cups or glasses garnished with the fruit.

Bloody Mary Mix

Without the vodka and vegetable sticks, this cost-cutting mix makes a delightful gift.

3 cups water
1 cup tomato juice
1 (6-oz.) can tomato paste
2 tablespoons chopped, seeded,
   peeled canned whole green chilies
2 tablespoons dried onion flakes
2 tablespoons vinegar
2 tablespoons Worcestershire sauce
1 tablespoon lemon juice

1 teaspoon celery salt
1 teaspoon salt
1 teaspoon sugar
1/4 teaspoon garlic powder
Hot pepper sauce to taste
Ice cubes
Vodka, if desired
Cucumber sticks or celery sticks

In blender container, mix water, tomato juice, tomato paste, green chilies, onion flakes, vinegar, Worcestershire sauce, lemon juice, celery salt, salt, sugar and garlic powder. Cover and process with blender on high speed until smooth, about 1-1/2 minutes. Season to taste with bottled hot pepper sauce. Serve over ice cubes. Stir 1 jigger of vodka into each glass, if desired. Garnish with cucumber sticks or celery sticks as stirrers. Makes 5 servings.

Salty Dogs

The perfect match for Mexican Egg Cups, page 65.

Lime juice
Salt
1 (46-oz.) can unsweetened grapefruit juice
1-1/2 cups vodka

1 tablespoon powdered sugar
Ice cubes
Lime slices

Dip the rims of 8 stemmed glasses in lime juice, then in salt. In a large pitcher, mix grapefruit juice, vodka and powdered sugar. Stir to dissolve sugar. To serve, pour grapefruit mixture over ice cubes in prepared glasses. Garnish with lime slices. Makes 8 servings.

Spiked Milk Punch

If you prefer a slushy drink, put it in the freezer for 4 hours after blending.

3/4 cup milk
3/4 cup half-and-half
6 tablespoons white crème de cacao
2 tablespoons brandy

4 teaspoons powdered sugar
1 egg white
Chocolate shavings

In blender container, mix milk, half-and-half, crème de cacao, brandy, powdered sugar and egg white. Cover and process with blender on high speed until frothy. Serve immediately in stemmed glasses. Garnish with chocolate shavings. Makes 4 servings.

Appetizers & Soups

Nibbling highly flavored foods is an ideal way to start a meal because they stimulate hunger without satiating the appetite.

When you plan the menu, be sure most of the foods have universal appeal so those guests who are not very adventurous will have a wide choice. But if you are serving two or more appetizers, introduce at least one food or dish which will be a novelty. If you've planned a hearty brunch, keep the appetizers light. If the meal is going to be fairly light, you can concentrate on heartier hors d'oeuvres.

Cold soups, chilled overnight to bring out their flavors, are impressive first courses. Gazpacho, the cold Spanish soup, is especially popular. For a hot soup designed for picnics, try Thermos Jug Soup. It's on page 17 in the menu section. It was created for a picnic, but don't let that stop you from serving it at home in your dining room.

Quiches are delicious appetizers. A 9-inch quiche can be cut to make 10 or 12 appetizer wedges; see Quiches, Omeletes & Soufflés, pages 49 to 52 and Appetizer Ham Quiches, page 15.

When pasta is served at an American meal, it is usually brought out with the entrée or main dish. When you serve Straw & Hay, which is green and white linguine combined in a creamy vegetable sauce, you're following the Italian tradition of serving pasta before the main dish.

Curried Chicken Rounds

Marvelous flavor! Chutney is the finishing touch.

1 (5-oz.) can boned chicken, undrained
1/2 cup shredded Swiss cheese (2 oz.)
1 (8-oz.) can water chestnuts,
   drained, finely diced
2 tablespoons finely chopped green onion
1/4 cup mayonnaise or salad dressing

1 teaspoon lemon juice
1/4 teaspoon curry powder
Dash pepper
1 (8-oz.) tube flaky-style refrigerated rolls
   (12 rolls)
3 tablespoons chutney

Preheat oven to 400°F (205°C). In a medium bowl, mix chicken, Swiss cheese, water chestnuts, green onion, mayonnaise, lemon juice, curry powder and pepper. Separate each roll into 3 layers. Place on an ungreased baking sheet. Spoon 1/2 tablespoon chicken mixture on each round. Top with 1/4 teaspoon chutney. Bake 10 minutes or until brown. Serve hot. Makes 36 appetizers.

Straw & Hay

This divine Italian appetizer can double as a main-dish of three or four servings.

4 oz. white linguine (2-1/2 cups)
4 oz. green linguine (2-1/2 cups)
Boiling salted water
1/2 cup butter or margarine
8 oz. cooked ham, cut in thin strips
   (1-1/2 cups)

3/4 cup cooked peas
1 (2-1/2-oz.) jar sliced mushrooms, drained
2 egg yolks, well beaten
1 cup whipping cream
1 cup freshly grated Parmesan cheese (4 oz.)

In a 6-quart heavy pot or Dutch oven, cook white and green linguine in boiling salted water until just tender. Drain and return linguine to pot. Add butter or margarine, ham, peas and mushrooms. In a small bowl, beat egg yolks and cream with a fork or whisk until foamy. Slowly add cream mixture to linguine, mixing well. Stir in 1/2 cup Parmesan cheese. Stir gently over medium-high heat, until mixture is thickened. Serve on individual plates. Sprinkle with remaining Parmesan cheese. Makes 6 appetizer servings.

Fresh Artichokes Vinaigrette

Prepare this fanciful appetizer a day ahead and assemble it just before serving.

6 fresh artichokes
Water
1 tablespoon lemon juice
1 tablespoon vegetable oil

1 teaspoon salt
2 garlic cloves
Shrimp Filling, see below

Shrimp Filling:
1 cup vegetable oil
2/3 cup white wine tarragon vinegar
2 (.6-oz.) pkgs. Italian salad dressing mix

3 cups shelled deveined cooked shrimp
   (about 7-1/2 oz.)

Cut stem and 1 inch from top of each artichoke. Snip off tips of leaves with scissors. In a large pot, combine water to cover artichokes, lemon juice, oil, salt and garlic. Bring to a boil. Add artichokes. Reduce heat. Cover and simmer 20 to 30 minutes or until an artichoke leaf pulls out easily. Drain and cool. Scoop out and discard choke. Chill artichokes. Prepare Shrimp Filling. Before serving, drain filling, reserving dressing. Spoon filling into center of artichokes and stuff randomly in between leaves, using about 1/2 cup filling for each artichoke. Drizzle with reserved dressing. Makes 6 appetizer servings.

Shrimp Filling:
In a screw-top jar, mix oil, vinegar and salad dressing mix. Shake well. Place shrimp in a shallow dish. Pour dressing over shrimp. Cover and chill. Makes 3 cups filling.

Spicy Miniature Sausage Balls

Get out your chafing dish to keep this attractive appetizer hot.

1 (8-oz.) can chunk pineapple (juice pack)
Water
1 lb. ground beef
12 oz. bulk pork sausage
1 cup herb-seasoned stuffing mix
1 (8-oz.) can water chestnuts, drained, minced

1/4 cup finely chopped onion
3 tablespoons grated Parmesan cheese
1/2 teaspoon garlic salt
Dash pepper
1 cup jumbo stuffed green olives
1 cup pickled mushrooms

Preheat oven to 375°F (190°C). Drain pineapple juice into a measuring cup; set pineapple aside. Add water to juice to make 1/3 cup liquid. In a large bowl, mix ground beef, sausage, pineapple juice mixture, stuffing mix, water chestnuts, onion, Parmesan cheese, garlic salt and pepper. Shape into 1-inch balls, using about 1 tablespoon meat mixture for each ball. Place in two 15" x 10" baking pans. Bake 15 to 20 minutes. Divide pineapple chunks, olives and mushrooms between baking pans. Bake 5 minutes or until meatballs are done and pineapple, olives and mushrooms are heated through. Drain. Serve with cocktail picks. Makes 48 appetizers.

Flaky Cheese Triangles

Freeze the baked pastries, then reheat them at 375°F (190°C) for 10 minutes.

Cheese Filling, see below
1/2 lb. frozen filo leaves thawed

1 cup butter or margarine, melted

Cheese Filling:
1/2 cup ricotta cheese
1 (4-oz.) container semisoft natural cheese
spiced with garlic and herbs

1/4 cup grated Parmesan cheese
2 eggs, well beaten

Prepare Cheese Filling; set aside. Cut filo leaves lengthwise in 2-1/2-inch wide strips. Stack and place strips between barely dampened cloth towels to prevent drying. Preheat oven to 375°F (190°C). Brush a strip of filo with melted butter or margarine. Place 1/2 tablespoon Cheese Filling on bottom corner of the strip. Fold corner with filling over, enclosing filling and forming a triangle at the bottom of the strip. Continue to fold the strip flag-fashion, maintaining the triangular shape. Place seam-side down on baking sheet. Brush with melted butter or margarine. Repeat with remaining filo strips. Bake 20 minutes or until browned and crisp. Makes 54 appetizers.

Cheese Filling:
In a small bowl, beat ricotta cheese and spiced natural cheese with electric mixer on medium speed until combined. Beat in Parmesan cheese and eggs.

Herbed Parmesan Puffs

These airy tidbits are easy with frozen patty shell dough.

1 (10-oz.) pkg. frozen ready-to-bake
   patty shells, thawed
1 egg, slightly beaten
1/2 cup grated Parmesan cheese

2 teaspoons sesame seeds
1 teaspoon parsley flakes, crushed
1 teaspoon celery salt
1/2 teaspoon dried thyme, crushed

Preheat oven to 425°F (220°C). Slightly overlap patty shells on a lightly floured board. Roll out to an 18" x 9" rectangle. Brush with beaten egg. Sprinkle half of pastry with 2 tablespoons Parmesan cheese; fold other half over to make a square. Roll out to a 16" x 12" rectangle. Brush with beaten egg and sprinkle with remaining Parmesan cheese. Combine sesame seeds, parsley flakes, celery salt and thyme; sprinkle evenly over cheese. With a sharp knife or pastry cutter, cut pastry lengthwise into 1-inch wide strips; then cut crosswise to make 1-inch squares. Place squares on ungreased baking sheets. Bake 9 to 10 minutes or until puffed and golden brown. Serve warm. Or cool and store in an airtight container in a cool place. Or cool, wrap and freeze. To reheat, place thawed puffs on a baking sheet and heat at 375°F (190°C) for 5 minutes. Makes about 120 appetizers.

Ham & Asparagus Puffs

For dessert cream puffs, make the puffs larger and fill them with your favorite dessert filling.

1 cup water
1/2 cup butter or margarine
1/4 teaspoon salt

1 cup all-purpose flour
4 eggs
Ham & Asparagus Filling, see below

Ham & Asparagus Filling:
1/2 cup mayonnaise or salad dressing
2 tablespoons butter or margarine, softened
1 tablespoon lemon juice
1 cup ground fully cooked ham

1 (10-oz.) pkg. frozen chopped asparagus,
   cooked, drained, finely chopped
1/4 cup finely chopped onion
Dash pepper

Preheat oven to 400°F (205°C). Grease 2 baking sheets; set aside. In a medium saucepan, mix water, butter or margarine and salt. Bring to a boil; stir in flour. Reduce heat to low. Stir constantly over low heat, until mixture forms a ball. Remove from heat and cool 4 minutes. Add eggs 1 at a time beating well after each addition. Drop dough by rounded teaspoonfuls onto the greased baking sheets to make 36 puffs. Bake 25 to 30 minutes or until puffed and golden. Cool on rack; split. Prepare Ham & Asparagus Filling. Spoon about 1 tablespoon filling into each puff. Makes 36 appetizers.

Ham & Asparagus Filling:
In a small bowl, mix mayonnaise, butter or margarine and lemon juice. Beat with electric mixer on medium speed until blended. Stir in ham, asparagus, onion and pepper.

Hot Cheese Dip With Pita Bread Dippers

Guaranteed to disappear in a hurry!

4 pita breads
1/4 cup butter or margarine, melted
Salad seasoning
1 (8-oz.) pkg. cream cheese, softened
1 cup shredded sharp process
   American cheese (4 oz.)

1/4 cup dry white wine
2 tablespoons milk
1/4 teaspoon garlic powder
1/4 cup finely chopped stuffed green olives

Preheat broiler to moderate temperature. Cut pita bread in 2-inch pieces. Place on rack in broiler pan. Generously brush pita pieces with melted butter or margarine. Sprinkle with salad seasoning. Broil 3 inches from heat about 2 minutes or until lightly browned. In a medium saucepan, place cream cheese, American cheese, wine, milk and garlic powder. Stir constantly over low heat until blended. Stir in olives. Pour into a small chafing dish and keep hot over a low flame. Add more milk if mixture becomes too thick. Serve with hot pita bread dippers. Makes 1-3/4 cups sauce.

Deep-Fried Cheese Bites

Cook these creamy delights in your wok or in a deep heavy skillet or saucepan.

Vegetable oil for deep frying
8 oz. Cheddar cheese
1/3 cup flour

1 egg, well beaten
1 cup cracker meal

Heat oil for deep frying to 375°F (190°C). At this temperature a 1-inch cube of bread dropped into oil will turn golden brown in 1 minute. While oil is heating, cut cheese in 1/2" x 1/2" x 3" sticks. Dip each stick in flour, then in egg, then in cracker meal to coat all sides. Fry cheese, a few pieces at a time, in hot oil 45 seconds to 1 minute or until well browned. Drain on paper towels. Serve immediately. Makes 36 appetizers.

Spinach Soufflé Mixture

One package of frozen spinach soufflé makes stuffing for two appetizers, see page 40.

1 (12-oz.) pkg. frozen spinach soufflé,
   thawed

1/3 cup seasoned breadcrumbs
1/3 cup grated Parmesan cheese

In a medium bowl, combine spinach soufflé, breadcrumbs and Parmesan cheese; mix well. Use to make Oyster Pastries Florentine and Stuffed Mushrooms Florentine. Makes about 1-3/4 cups.

Bloody Mary Appetizer Molds

Use non-alcoholic beverage mix to make an interesting molded salad.

2 envelopes unflavored gelatin
3-3/4 cups bottled non-alcoholic
   Bloody Mary mix
1 cup chopped, seeded, peeled cucumber
1 cup chopped celery

1/2 cup chopped green pepper
1/2 cup chopped green onion
Celery leaves
Green Onion Fans, see below

In a large saucepan, soften gelatin in 1 cup Bloody Mary mix. Stir constantly over low heat until gelatin dissolves. Stir in remaining Bloody Mary mix. Refrigerate until partially set. Fold in cucumber, celery, green pepper and green onion. Spoon into 8 wine glasses or sherbet dishes. Refrigerate until firm, 8 hours or overnight. Garnish with celery leaves and Green Onion Fans. Makes 8 appetizer servings.

How To Make
Bloody Mary Appetizer Molds

1/To dissolve plain gelatin in Bloody Mary mix, stir over low heat. Refrigerate until partially set as in the photo. The mixture will hold its shape when spooned. The chopped vegetables will stay more evenly distributed if they are folded in at the partially set stage.

2/To make Green Onion Fans, cut the white end of green onions into 2 or 3 inch lengths. Make 2 or 3 slits from each end of the onion almost to the center. Give onion 1/4 turn and repeat cutting. Chill in ice water until the onions open to form fans.

Stuffed Mushrooms Florentine

Fill Oyster Pastries Florentine, below with the remaining Spinach Soufflé Mixture.

1 cup Spinach Soufflé Mixture, page 38
14 to 16 large (1-1/2 to 2-inch diameter)
   mushrooms

1/4 cup butter or margarine, melted
Seasoned breadcrumbs, page 77

Set prepared Spinach Soufflé Mixture aside. Preheat oven to 400°F (205°C). Remove stems from mushrooms and reserve for another use. Rinse mushrooms and pat dry. Dip in melted butter or margarine. Place upside down in a shallow baking dish. Stuff mushroom caps with Spinach Soufflé Mixture, using about 1 tablespoonful for each mushroom. Drizzle with any remaining melted butter or margarine. Top each mushroom with a few seasoned breadcrumbs. Bake 15 minutes or until soufflé mixture is done. Makes 14 to 16 appetizers.

Oyster Pastries Florentine

Use the remaining Spinach Soufflé Mixture to make Stuffed Mushrooms Florentine, above.

About 3/4 cup Spinach Soufflé Mixture,
   page 38
3 sticks pastry mix
Water

6 tablespoons shredded Swiss cheese
6 large or 12 small fresh shucked oysters
3 tablespoons butter or margarine, melted
Thin lemon slices, quartered

Set prepared Spinach Soufflé Mixture aside. Preheat oven to 400°F (205°C). Prepare pastry mix with water according to package directions. On a lightly floured surface, roll out 1/8 inch thick. Cut into 4-1/2- to 5-inch rounds. Fit into twelve 3-1/2-inch round appetizer quiche pans. Or turn up and crimp edges and place pastries directly on a baking sheet. Trim off excess dough even with edges of pans. Do not prick dough. Place pans on a baking sheet. Bake 4 to 5 minutes or until lightly browned. Cool slightly. Remove shells from pans; place on baking sheet. Increase oven temperature to 425°F (220°C). Spoon about 1/2 tablespoon Swiss cheese into bottom of each pastry shell. Pat oysters dry on paper towels; halve, if large. Dip oysters in melted butter or margarine and place on cheese in pastry shells. Drizzle with any remaining butter. Top each oyster with 1 tablespoon Spinach Soufflé Mixture. Bake 10 minutes or until heated through. Garnish with lemon triangles. Serve hot. Makes 12 appetizers.

Stuffed Mushroom Caps

For a large brunch, use 40 mushrooms; stuff half with shrimp and half with sausage.

Sausage Stuffing For Mushroom Caps or
   Shrimp Stuffing For Mushroom Caps, below

20 large (2-inch diameter) mushrooms

Remove stems from mushrooms and reserve for another use. Preheat broiler at moderate temperature. Prepare Sausage or Shrimp Stuffing. Stuff mushroom caps, using about 1 tablespoon stuffing for each cap. Place stuffed mushrooms on a broiler pan. Broil 3 to 4 inches from the heat 2 to 3 minutes, until heated through. Makes 20 appetizers or 4 main-dish servings.

Sausage Stuffing For Mushroom Caps

Serve Stuffed Mushroom Caps with this stuffing as a main dish for a small group.

8 oz. bulk pork sausage
1/4 cup finely chopped onion
1/4 cup finely chopped green pepper
2 tablespoons chopped pimiento

1 teaspoon dried oregano
1/8 teaspoon garlic powder
1/8 teaspoon pepper
1/2 cup dairy sour cream

In a medium skillet, combine all ingredients except sour cream. Stir constantly over medium-high heat until sausage is done. Remove from heat; drain. Stir sour cream into sausage mixture. Use to make Stuffed Mushroom Caps. Makes about 1-1/4 cups.

Shrimp Stuffing For Mushroom Caps

Crush the crackers in a sturdy plastic bag with a rolling pin.

1 cup chopped cooked shrimp
1/2 cup finely crushed Ritz crackers
1/4 cup grated Parmesan cheese
2 tablespoons butter or margarine, melted

1 tablespoon snipped parsley
2 teaspoons snipped chives
1/2 teaspoon seasoned salt
1/8 teaspoon garlic powder

In a small bowl, thoroughly mix all ingredients. Use to make Stuffed Mushroom Caps. Makes about 1-1/4 cups.

Liver Pâté Royale

Don't let this classic scare you—it's easy enough for a beginner!

2 cups water	1 teaspoon salt
2 teaspoons instant chicken bouillon granules	1/2 teaspoon dry mustard
1 lb. chicken livers	1/4 teaspoon dried thyme
2 tablespoons chopped onion	1/4 teaspoon ground allspice
4 tablespoons butter or margarine, softened	4 bay leaves
2 tablespoons mayonnaise or salad dressing	Watercress, if desired
2 tablespoons cognac or brandy	Assorted crackers

Oil a 3-cup mold or a small bowl; set aside. In a medium saucepan, mix water and bouillon granules. Add chicken livers. Bring to a boil. Reduce heat. Cover and simmer 15 to 20 minutes or until livers are no longer pink in the centers. Drain. Put livers and onion through the finest blade of a food grinder. Stir butter or margarine, mayonnaise or salad dressing, cognac or brandy, salt, dry mustard, thyme and allspice into liver mixture. Arrange bay leaves in bottom of the oiled mold. Pack liver mixture in mold. Cover mold with foil. Place a heavy bowl on top of foil to weigh down mixture. Refrigerate several hours or overnight. If desired, arrange watercress on platter. Turn mixture out of mold onto platter. Serve with assorted crackers. Makes 4 to 6 appetizer servings.

Sesame Cheese Twists

Spread leftover cheese mixture on slices of French bread and broil until cheese is bubbling.

4 tablespoons butter or margarine, softened	Water
1/2 (5-oz.) jar sharp process cheese food	Sesame seeds
1 stick pie crust mix	

Preheat oven to 450°F (230°C). In a small bowl, beat butter or margarine and cheese with electric mixer on high speed until fluffy. Prepare pie crust mix with water according to package directions. On a lightly floured board, roll out dough to a 12" x 8" rectangle. Cut crosswise to make two 6" x 8" rectangles. Spread 1/4 cup of the cheese mixture on 1 rectangle. Top with remaining rectangle. Spread 1/4 cup of the cheese mixture on second rectangle. Sprinkle with sesame seeds. Cut crosswise to form eight 3/4-inch strips. Cut each strip in half crosswise. Twist each strip 3 times. Place on an ungreased baking sheet. Bake 10 to 12 minutes. Makes 16 appetizers.

Vichyssoise

Not really French, vichyssoise was created by the chef at New York's Ritz-Carlton Hotel in 1910.

2 leeks (1-1/4 lbs.)
1 medium onion, chopped (1 cup)
1-1/3 cups water
4 teaspoons instant chicken bouillon granules
1/4 to 1/2 teaspoon salt

1-1/2 cups instant potato flakes
2-1/3 cups milk
1 cup whipping cream
Snipped chives

Chop white part of leeks; discard tops. In a large saucepan, mix leeks, onion, water, bouillon granules and salt. Bring to a boil over high heat. Reduce heat. Cover and simmer 10 minutes. Pour mixture into blender container. Add potato flakes and 2/3 cup milk. Cover and process with blender on high speed until smooth. Pour into a large bowl. Stir in remaining 1-2/3 cups milk and whipping cream. Force mixture through a fine sieve. Cover and refrigerate 8 hours or overnight. Serve cold with a sprinkling of chives. Makes 8 servings.

Swiss Corn Chowder

If you prefer a smooth consistency, process this soup in your blender and reheat before serving.

12 slices bacon
1/2 cup chopped green pepper
1/2 cup chopped onion
1/3 cup all-purpose flour
1 teaspoon celery salt
1/4 teaspoon pepper

4 cups half-and-half
1/4 cup chopped pimiento
2 (10-oz.) pkgs. frozen whole
　　kernel corn, thawed
2 cups shredded process Swiss cheese (8 oz.)
Snipped chives

Preheat broiler at moderate temperature. Place bacon on broiler pan. Broil 3 to 4 inches from heat until crisp. Remove bacon and crumble, reserving 1/4 cup drippings. In a 4-quart Dutch oven or heavy pot, cook green pepper and onion in reserved bacon drippings over medium-high heat, until tender, stirring occasionally. Blend in flour, celery salt and pepper. Stir in half-and-half and pimiento. Stir constantly over medium-high heat until mixture thickens and bubbles. Stir in corn and cheese. Bring to a boil. Reduce heat. Cover and simmer 20 minutes or until corn is tender, stirring occasionally. Ladle into small bowls. Sprinkle with crumbled bacon and snipped chives. Makes 8 to 10 appetizer servings.

Serve cold soups in chilled bowls or in bowls which are placed over crushed ice in a larger bowl. On particularly festive occasions, serve cold soups in chilled glasses.

Creamy Avocado Soup

Select only ripe flavorful avocados for this elegant soup.

1 (13-3/4-oz.) can chicken broth
3 ripe avocados, peeled, cut in chunks
1/4 cup chopped green onion
1/4 teaspoon chili powder

1/4 teaspoon ground coriander
1/8 teaspoon white pepper
1 cup half-and-half
Avocado slices

In blender container, place chicken broth, avocado chunks, green onion, chili powder, coriander and white pepper. Cover and process with blender on high speed until smooth. Pour mixture into a medium saucepan. Cook over medium heat, stirring occasionally, until mixture just boils. Remove from heat and stir in half-and-half. Cover and refrigerate. Serve cold topped with avocado slices. Makes 6 servings.

Gazpacho

This Spanish soup is always served cold.

1 cup finely chopped, seeded,
  peeled tomato
1 cup chopped, seeded cucumber
3/4 cup chopped green onion
3/4 cup chopped celery
3/4 cup sliced black olives
1 (10-1/2-oz.) can condensed beef broth

3 cups tomato juice
1/2 cup dry white wine
3 tablespoons red wine vinegar
1/4 teaspoon garlic powder
1/4 teaspoon hot pepper sauce
Cucumber sticks or celery sticks, if desired

In a large bowl, mix tomato, cucumber, green onion, celery, black olives, beef broth, tomato juice, wine, vinegar, garlic powder and hot pepper sauce. Cover and refrigerate several hours or overnight. Serve cold. Garnish with cucumber sticks or celery sticks, if desired. Makes 8 servings.

Clear Mushroom Soup

Top this delicate soup with croutons to add a contrasting texture.

1 cup sliced fresh mushrooms
2 to 4 tablespoons chopped shallots or
  green onion

3/4 cup dry white wine
2 (13-3/4-oz.) cans chicken broth

In a medium saucepan, mix mushrooms, shallots or green onion and wine. Cook uncovered over medium heat until liquid is reduced by half, a little more than 1/3 cup. Stir in chicken broth. Heat through. Serve hot. Makes 6 appetizer servings.

Sorrel Bisque

Sorrel or sour grapes *is a perennial herb with a slightly lemony taste.*

1 (10-oz.) pkg. frozen chopped broccoli
1 (13-3/4-oz.) can chicken broth
1 (8-oz.) can tomato sauce
1 cup fresh sorrel or spinach, chopped
1 medium onion, sliced
1 stalk celery, sliced

1 carrot, peeled, sliced
1 teaspoon salt
2 teaspoons Worcestershire sauce
1/2 cup dairy sour cream
Snipped chives

In a large saucepan, mix broccoli, chicken broth, tomato sauce, sorrel, onion, celery, carrot, salt and Worcestershire sauce. Bring to a boil. Reduce heat. Cover and simmer 15 minutes or until vegetables are tender. Pour half the mixture into a blender container. Cover and process with blender on high speed until smooth. Pour into a glass or plastic bowl. Repeat with remaining half of mixture. Add to mixture in bowl, cover and refrigerate 6 hours or overnight. To serve, ladle into small bowls. Top with a dollop of sour cream and a sprinkling of chives. Makes 6 servings.

How To Make Sorrel Bisque

1/Simmer fresh sorrel with vegetables and broth. Blend 1/2 the mixture at a time then chill. If you're not familiar with sorrel, it looks much like spinach, as you can see in the orange colander.

2/After chilling thoroughly, serve the bisque in small bowls. Garnish each serving with a dollop of sour cream and a sprinkling of snipped fresh chives.

Double-Cheese Chowder

Close the generation gap with popcorn croutons in each bowl of soup.

1/2 cup butter or margarine
1 cup chopped onion
1/2 cup shredded carrot
1/2 cup chopped celery
3/4 cup all-purpose flour
2 teaspoons paprika
1 teaspoon dry mustard

1 teaspoon Worcestershire sauce
1/4 teaspoon pepper
2 cups chicken broth
2-1/2 cups half-and-half
6 oz. cold pack sharp Cheddar cheese food
1-1/2 cups shredded Cheddar cheese (6 oz.)
Buttered popcorn

In a large saucepan, melt butter or margarine. Add onion, carrot and celery. Cook over medium-high heat 5 minutes, stirring occasionally. Blend in flour, paprika, dry mustard, Worcestershire sauce and pepper. Stir in chicken broth. Stir constantly over medium-high heat until mixture thickens and bubbles. Reduce heat. Stir in half-and-half and cheeses. Simmer over low heat 15 minutes, stirring occasionally. Ladle into small bowls. Sprinkle with buttered popcorn. Makes 6 appetizer servings.

Garlic Cheese Soup

This stand-out owes its success to the spiced cheese.

4 tablespoons butter or margarine
3 tablespoons all-purpose flour
1 tablespoon snipped chives
1 teaspoon paprika
1/2 teaspoon dry mustard
1/4 teaspoon salt

Dash pepper
1 (13-3/4-oz.) can chicken broth
2 cups half-and-half
2 (4-oz.) containers semisoft natural cheese
   spiced with garlic and herbs

In a large heavy saucepan, melt butter or margarine. Blend in flour, chives, paprika, dry mustard, salt and pepper. Add chicken broth and half-and-half. Stir constantly over medium-high heat until mixture thickens and bubbles. Reduce heat to low. Add cheese. Stir until melted. Makes 6 servings.

Quiches, Omelets & Souffles

Quiche is a flavorful custard baked in a pastry shell. It is supposed to have originated in Lorraine, a French province, and so the best known of these custards is Quiche Lorraine.

Do not prick a quiche crust before baking or the crust will become soggy from the egg mixture. Use one of these methods to prevent the crust from shrinking and raising: Fold 2 pieces of foil to make two 11" x 2" strips. Place the strips on the crust to make an X which extends over the crust rim. Place another pie plate on top of the foil and bake the crust following prebaking directions in the crust recipe. When the crust is done lift the foil strips to remove the top plate. The crust is ready to be filled. Another method is to prebake the crust filled with dried beans on foil. This is called *baking blind*. Remove the beans before filling the crust with the quiche mixture.

When a large 9- or 10-inch diameter quiche is done, a knife inserted off-center, halfway between the center and edge of the quiche should come out clean—no egg mixture clinging to the knife. Push the knife only about 2/3 of the way down into the filling or it will meet the sticky cheese layer at the bottom. The center of the quiche continues to cook during the 10-minute standing time. To test a smaller 2- or 3-inch diameter quiche, insert the knife directly into the center. Because the quiche is so small, very little cooking will occur after it is removed from the oven.

Quiches can be served as either main dishes or appetizers. A 9- or 10-inch quiche makes 6 to 8 main dish servings or 10 to 12 appetizer servings.

Omelets are made by combining eggs, milk or water, salt, pepper and often herbs. Omelets may be puffed, with the yolks and whites beaten separately, or made the traditional French way with the yolks and whites beaten together. French-style omelets may be flat or folded or rolled over a filling.

The Italian *frittata*, see page 68 is an omelet made with vegetables and browned on both sides. The Spanish *tortilla*, see page 70 is cooked until one side is crisp and it is usually served in wedges. Don't confuse the Spanish *tortilla* or omelet with Mexican *tortillas* which are a kind of flat bread made with corn.

Special omelet pans have sloping sides to help contain the swirling egg mixture and make it easy to slip the omelet out onto a plate. If you don't own an omelet pan, don't despair—you can make a satisfactory omelet in any small skillet.

Soufflés are a combination of a thick sauce, eggs and ingredients such as cheese, broccoli, crab or chocolate for flavor. There are two basic kinds of soufflés: Main dish soufflés are made with seafood, cheese or vegetables. Dessert soufflés usually have chocolate, fruit or liqueur added.

If you've shied away from making a soufflé because you thought it would be too difficult to do in the last-minute rush, here's a tip. Make the cream sauce or base about two hours before you plan to serve it. Cover it and let it stand. About an hour before serving time, fold in the beaten egg whites and your soufflé is ready to bake. See the discussions on beating egg whites, pages 63, 65 and 141.

Once baking begins, don't open the oven door; temperature and pressure need to be constant.

The timings in this book will yield a soufflé which is set up or firm all the way through. If you want to serve a soufflé European fashion, slightly underbake it, then spoon the unset center as a sauce over the soufflé servings.

To serve a firm soufflé, hold two forks back to back—one fork in each hand. Gently insert the forks into the center of the soufflé and pull apart slightly, working toward the edge of the souffle. Do this until the soufflé has been divided into serving-size wedges. Gently lift servings onto plates with a large spoon to retain as much of the delicately puffed texture as possible.

Individual Frozen Swiss Soufflés are on page 12. Recipes for dessert soufflés are in Desserts, pages 146 to 148.

Tostada Quiche

Display your Mexican souvenirs and enjoy this colorful one-dish fiesta.

1 (9-inch) frozen deep-dish pastry shell
2 avocados, peeled, seeded, mashed
1 garlic clove, minced
3 tablespoons lemon juice
1 tomato, peeled, seeded, chopped
1 (4-oz.) can whole green chilies,
    seeded, chopped
1/4 teaspoon hot pepper sauce
8 oz. ground beef
1/4 cup chopped onion

1 to 2 tablespoons taco seasoning mix
1-1/2 cups shredded Cheddar cheese (6 oz.)
3 eggs, slightly beaten
1-1/2 cups half-and-half
1/2 teaspoon salt
1/8 teaspoon pepper
Shredded lettuce
Corn chips
Chopped tomato

Preheat oven to 400°F (205°C). Let frozen pastry shell stand at room temperature 10 minutes; do not prick the pastry shell. In a small bowl, mix avocados, garlic and lemon juice. Stir in 1 chopped tomato, 1 tablespoon green chilies and hot pepper sauce. Cover and refrigerate. Bake pastry shell 7 minutes. Remove from oven; set aside. Reduce oven temperature to 375°F (190°C). In a medium skillet, combine ground beef, onion, remaining green chilies and taco seasoning mix. Cook over medium-high heat, stirring occasionally, until ground beef is browned and onion is tender. Drain ground beef mixture. Layer cheese and then ground beef mixture in the pastry shell. In a medium bowl, combine eggs, half-and-half, salt and pepper. Beat with a fork or whisk until mixed well but not frothy. Pour egg mixture over ground beef mixture. Bake 45 minutes or until a knife inserted off-center comes out clean. Let stand 10 minutes before serving. Garnish with shredded lettuce, tomato and avocado mixture. Or place dishes or shredded lettuce, corn chips, additional chopped tomato and the avocado mixture on the table for your guests. Makes 6 servings.

French Fried Onion Quiche *Photo on page 5.*

Serve small wedges of this quiche with Herb-Buttered Breakfast Steaks, page 94.

1 (9-inch) frozen deep-dish pastry shell
1-1/2 cups shredded Swiss cheese (6 oz.)
1 (3-oz.) can French fried onions (2 cups)
3 eggs, slightly beaten
1-1/2 cups half-and-half

1/2 teaspoon salt
1/8 teaspoon pepper
Paprika
Dairy sour cream

Preheat oven to 400°F (205°C). Let frozen pastry shell stand at room temperature 10 minutes; do not prick the pastry shell. Bake 7 minutes. Remove from oven. Reduce oven temperature to 375°F (190°C). Sprinkle first the cheese and then 1-1/3 cups French fried onions in the pastry shell. In a medium bowl, combine eggs, half-and-half, salt and pepper. Beat with a fork or whisk until mixed well but not frothy. Pour egg mixture over onions and cheese in pastry shell. Sprinkle with paprika. Bake 45 minutes or until a knife inserted off-center comes out clean. Let stand 10 minutes before serving. Top with sour cream and remaining onions. Makes 6 servings.

Quiche Italiano

If you prick the pastry shells, you will probably have a quiche with a soggy crust.

2 sticks pie crust mix
Water
2-1/2 oz. pepperoni, sliced (1/2 cup)
3 tablespoons chopped green pepper
2 tablespoons chopped onion
1 (2-1/2-oz.) jar sliced mushrooms, drained
1 tablespoon butter or margarine
1/2 teaspoon crushed dried oregano

1/2 teaspoon fennel seeds
1 cup shredded mozzarella cheese (4 oz.)
3 eggs
1-1/2 cups half-and-half
1/2 teaspoon salt
1/8 teaspoon pepper
1 tomato, cut in wedges
1/4 cup shredded mozzarella cheese (1 oz.)

Preheat oven to 400°F (205°C). Prepare pie crust mix with water according to package directions. Roll out 1/8 inch thick on a lightly floured surface. Cut into four 7-inch rounds. Fit into 4 (1-cup) 5-inch individual quiche dishes. Trim edges; do not prick the pastry shells. Bake 5 to 7 minutes. Remove from oven; set aside. Reduce oven temperature to 375°F (190°C). In a small skillet, cook pepperoni, green pepper, onion and mushrooms in butter or margarine until tender. Stir in oregano and fennel seeds. Layer 1/4 cup mozzarella cheese in each pastry shell. Top each with an equal amount of pepperoni mixture. In a medium bowl, combine eggs, half-and-half, salt and pepper. Beat with a fork or whisk until mixed well but not frothy. Pour equally over pepperoni mixture in each pastry. Bake 25 to 30 minutes or until knife inserted off-center comes out clean. Top with tomato wedges. Sprinkle each quiche with 1 tablespoon remaining mozzarella cheese. Bake 2 minutes longer or until cheese melts. Let stand 5 minutes before serving. Makes 4 servings.

Quiche Lorraine

This popular quiche has a reputation as successful brunch fare.

Basic Pastry, page 57
10 slices bacon (about 8 oz.)
1-1/2 cups shredded Swiss cheese (6 oz.)
1/2 cup finely chopped onion
1 (2-1/2-oz.) jar sliced mushrooms, drained

4 eggs, slightly beaten
2-1/2 cups half-and-half
1/2 teaspoon salt
1/8 teaspoon pepper
Dash ground nutmeg

Preheat oven to 400°F (205°C). Prepare Basic Pastry dough. Roll out dough on a lightly floured surface until it is about 3 inches larger than an inverted 9-1/2-inch quiche pan. Fit dough into the quiche pan. Trim edges, fold under and flute; do not prick the pastry shell. Bake 7 minutes. Remove from oven; set aside. Reduce oven temperature to 375°F (190°C). In a large skillet, cook bacon over medium-high heat until crisp. Drain and crumble bacon. Sprinkle first cheese, then bacon, onion and mushrooms in the pastry shell. In a medium bowl, combine eggs, half-and-half, salt, pepper and nutmeg. Beat with a fork or whisk until mixed well but not frothy. Pour egg mixture into pastry shell. Bake 50 to 55 minutes or until a knife inserted off-center comes out clean. Let stand 10 minutes before serving. Makes 8 servings.

Cheddar Ham Quiche

Serve with a wedge of melon or a few seedless grapes for a most refreshing brunch.

Basic Pastry, page 57
1 tablespoon vegetable oil
8 oz. fully cooked ham, cut in 1/4-inch
   cubes (about 1-1/3 cups)
1/2 cup finely chopped green pepper
1 tablespoon chopped pimiento

1-1/2 cups shredded Cheddar cheese (6 oz.)
3 eggs, slightly beaten
2 cups half-and-half
1/2 teaspoon salt
1/8 teaspoon pepper
Dash ground nutmeg

Preheat oven to 400°F (205°C). Prepare Basic Pastry dough. On a lightly floured board, roll out dough until it is about 2 inches larger than an inverted 10-inch pie plate. Fit dough into the pie plate. Trim edges, fold under and flute; do not prick the pastry shell. Bake 7 minutes. Remove from oven; set aside. Reduce oven temperature to 375°F (190°C). Heat oil in a medium skillet. Add ham, green pepper and pimiento. Cook over medium-high heat until green pepper is tender, stirring occasionally. Drain ham mixture. Sprinkle first cheese and then ham mixture in pastry shell. In a medium bowl, combine eggs, half-and-half, salt, pepper and nutmeg. Beat with a fork or whisk until well mixed but not frothy. Pour egg mixture over ham mixture in the pastry shell. Bake 45 minutes or until a knife inserted off-center comes out clean. Let stand 10 minutes before serving. Makes 6 servings.

Shrimp Boat Quiche

A frozen pastry shell cuts the preparation time for this colorful quiche.

1 (9-inch) frozen deep-dish pastry shell
1 tablespoon butter or margarine
1 cup chopped cooked shrimp
1/4 cup chopped onion
1/4 cup chopped pimiento
1-1/2 cups shredded Cheddar cheese (6 oz.)

3 eggs
1-1/2 cups half-and-half
1/2 teaspoon salt
1/8 teaspoon pepper
Snipped parsley
Paprika

Preheat oven to 400°F (205°C). Let the frozen pastry shell stand at room temperature for 10 minutes; do not prick the pastry shell. Bake 7 minutes. Remove from oven; set aside. Reduce oven temperature to 375°F (190°C). In a medium skillet, melt butter or margarine. Add shrimp, onion and pimiento. Cook over medium-high heat until onion is tender, stirring occasionally. Drain shrimp mixture. Sprinkle first cheese and then shrimp mixture in the pastry shell. In a medium bowl, combine eggs, half-and-half, salt and pepper. Beat with a fork or whisk until mixed well but not frothy. Pour egg mixture over shrimp mixture in the pastry shell. Sprinkle with snipped parsley and paprika. Bake 45 to 50 minutes or until a knife inserted off-center comes out clean. Let stand 10 minutes before serving. Makes 6 servings.

Spinach-Sausage Quiche

Don't pass this one by—it's absolutely delicious!

1 (9-inch) frozen deep-dish pastry shell
8 oz. bulk pork sausage
1/4 cup chopped green onion
1 garlic clove, minced
1/2 (10-oz.) pkg. frozen chopped spinach,
   cooked, drained well (about 5/8 cup)
1/2 cup herb-seasoned stuffing mix

1-1/2 cups shredded Monterey Jack cheese
   (6 oz.)
3 eggs, slightly beaten
1-1/2 cups half-and-half
2 tablespoons grated Parmesan cheese
Paprika

Preheat oven to 400°F (205°C). Let frozen pastry shell stand at room temperature 10 minutes; do not prick the pastry shell. Bake 7 minutes. Remove from oven; set aside. Reduce oven temperature to 375°F (190°C). In a medium skillet, cook sausage, green onion and garlic over medium-high heat until sausage is done, stirring occasionally. Drain sausage mixture. Stir in spinach and stuffing mix. Sprinkle first cheese and then sausage mixture in the pastry shell. In a medium bowl, combine eggs and half-and-half with a fork or whisk until mixed well but not frothy. Pour egg mixture over sausage mixture in the pastry shell. Bake 30 minutes. Sprinkle with Parmesan cheese and paprika. Bake 15 minutes or until a knife inserted off-center comes out clean. Let stand 10 minutes before serving. Makes 6 servings.

How To Make Spinach-Sausage Quiche

1/To use a frozen pastry shell in your own pie plate, let the frozen shell thaw at room temperature for 15 to 25 minutes, then transfer the crust carefully to your pie plate. Do not prick the crust; prebake for 7 minutes. Layer with cheese and the spinach mixture.

2/The egg and cream mixture should be smooth and blended but not frothy. Pour it into the quiche shell. Bake until a knife inserted off-center comes out clean. The quiche will not be completely set in the center but will finish cooking during the 10-minute standing time.

Basic French Omelet

Sprinkle on an herb or create your own extra-special filling.

4 eggs
2 tablespoons water
1/2 teaspoon salt

1/8 teaspoon pepper
2 tablespoons butter or margarine

In a small bowl, combine eggs, water, salt and pepper. Beat with a fork or whisk until mixed well but not frothy. In an 8-inch omelet pan or skillet, melt 1 tablespoon butter or margarine over medium-high heat. When a drop of water sizzles in the pan, pour in half the egg mixture. Cook, gently lifting edges so uncooked portion flows underneath, until eggs are set. Fold or roll omelet, place on a plate and serve immediately. Repeat with remaining egg mixture and butter or margarine. Makes 2 servings.

Fluffy Omelet With Cheddar Sauce

This delicate omelet is perfect for an intimate brunch.

Cheddar Sauce, see below
4 egg whites
2 tablespoons water

1/4 teaspoon salt
4 egg yolks
1 tablespoon butter or margarine

Cheddar Sauce:
1-1/2 tablespoons butter or margarine
1 tablespoon all-purpose flour
1/8 teaspoon dry mustard
1/8 teaspoon salt

Dash pepper
1/2 cup milk
1/4 cup shredded Cheddar cheese (2 oz.)

Prepare Cheddar Sauce; keep warm over low heat while preparing omelet. Preheat oven to 325°F (165°C). In a small bowl, beat egg whites with electric mixer on high speed until soft peaks form. Add water and salt. Beat until stiff peaks form. In another small bowl, beat egg yolks with electric mixer on high speed until thickened and lemon-colored, about 5 minutes. Slowly pour egg yolks over egg whites and gently fold together. In a 9-inch oven-proof skillet, melt butter or margarine over medium-high heat. When a drop of water sizzles in the pan, pour in egg mixture. Reduce heat to medium-low. Cook about 8 minutes or until omelet is puffed and bottom is browned. Place pan in oven and bake omelet about 10 minutes or until a knife inserted in center comes out clean. Remove omelet from skillet by running spatula around edges to loosen. Fold omelet in half and gently lift onto platter. Top with Cheddar Sauce. Makes 2 servings.

Cheddar Sauce:
In a small saucepan, melt butter or margarine. Stir in flour, dry mustard, salt and pepper. Add milk. Stir constantly over medium-high heat until mixture thickens and bubbles. Reduce heat to low and stir in cheese. Cook, stirring constantly, until cheese is melted. Makes 1/2 cup of sauce.

Zesty Ham Omelet

If you're a horseradish fan, here's the omelet for you.

4 tablespoons butter or margarine
2 cups frozen potatoes O'Brien, thawed
2 cups diced cooked ham
1/2 cup pasteurized Neufchatel cheese dip
 with bacon and horseradish
8 eggs
1/4 cup milk

1 teaspoon salt
1/4 teaspoon pepper
4 tablespoons butter or margarine
Pasteurized Neufchatel cheese dip
 with bacon and horseradish
Snipped chives

In a medium skillet, melt 4 tablespoons butter or margarine. Add potatoes and ham. Cook over medium-high heat until potatoes are tender, stirring occasionally. Stir in 1/2 cup cheese dip until blended. Keep warm over low heat while preparing omelets. In a medium bowl, combine eggs, milk, salt and pepper. Beat with a fork or whisk until mixed well but not frothy. In an 8-inch omelet pan or skillet, melt 1 tablespoon butter or margarine over medium-high heat. When a drop of water sizzles in the pan, pour in 1/4 of the egg mixture. Cook, gently lifting edges so uncooked portion flows underneath, until eggs are set. Spoon about 1/2 cup potato mixture onto omelet. Fold omelet and place on a plate. Garnish with additional cheese dip and snipped chives. Repeat with remaining butter or margarine, egg mixture and potato mixture to make 3 more omelets. Makes 4 servings.

Midsummer Night's Omelet

Rich cheese flavor with a pleasant blend of herbs and vegetables.

3 tablespoons butter or margarine
1 cup sliced zucchini
1 cup fresh corn
8 cherry tomatoes, halved
1/2 teaspoon dried thyme
1/2 teaspoon dried basil
1 (4-oz.) container semisoft natural
 cheese spiced with garlic and herbs

1 tablespoon milk
8 eggs
1/4 cup milk
1 teaspoon salt
1/4 teaspoon pepper
4 tablespoons butter or margarine
Dried thyme
Dried basil

In a medium skillet, melt 3 tablespoons butter or margarine. Add zucchini, corn, cherry tomatoes, 1/2 teaspoon thyme and 1/2 teaspoon basil. Cook over medium-high heat until vegetables are tender, stirring occasionally. Stir in cheese and 1 tablespoon milk. Mix gently until sauce is smooth. Keep warm over low heat while preparing omelets. In a medium bowl, mix eggs, remaining 1/4 cup milk, salt and pepper with a fork or whisk until just combined. In an 8-inch omelet pan or skillet, melt 1 tablespoon butter or margarine over medium-high heat. When a drop of water sizzles in the pan, pour in 1/4 of the egg mixture. Cook, gently lifting edges so uncooked portion flows underneath, until eggs are set. Spoon about 1/2 cup zucchini filling onto omelet. Fold omelet and place on a plate. Garnish with a spoonful of zucchini mixture and a sprinkling of thyme and basil. Serve immediately. Repeat with remaining butter or margarine, egg mixture and zucchini mixture to make 3 more omelets, sprinkling each with thyme and basil. Makes 4 servings.

Deluxe Vegetarian Omelet

Mix the eggs and milk thoroughly, but not so much that air is beaten into the mixture.

1/4 cup Italian salad dressing or
  clear French salad dressing
1/2 cup shredded carrot
1/4 cup chopped green onion
1/2 cup sliced, seeded, peeled cucumber
1 tomato, peeled, seeded, chopped
8 eggs

1/4 cup milk
1 teaspoon salt
1/4 teaspoon pepper
4 tablespoons butter or margarine
1 cup alfalfa sprouts
Plain yogurt
Snipped chives

In a small saucepan, combine salad dressing, carrot and onion. Cook over medium-high heat, until tender, stirring frequently. Stir in cucumber and tomato. Keep warm over low heat while preparing omelets. In a medium bowl, combine eggs, milk, salt and pepper. Beat with a fork or whisk until mixed well but not frothy. In an 8-inch omelet pan or skillet, melt 1 tablespoon butter or margarine over medium-high heat. When a drop of water sizzles in the pan, pour in 1/4 of the egg mixture. Cook, gently lifting edges so uncooked portion flows underneath, until eggs are set. Spoon about 1/2 cup of the vegetable mixture onto omelet and top with 1/4 cup alfalfa sprouts. Fold omelet and place on a plate. Garnish with a spoonful of yogurt and a sprinkling of chives. Serve immediately. Repeat with remaining butter or margarine, egg mixture and vegetable mixture to make 3 more omelets. Makes 4 servings.

How To Make Deluxe Vegetarian Omelet

1/The omelet is done when the top glistens and is barely set. Top half the omelet with vegetable filling and sprouts.

2/With a spatula, fold the other half of omelet over the filling and carefully place the filled, folded omelet on a plate.

Reuben Omelet

Perk up your brunch with this adaptation of the Reuben sandwich.

2 tablespoons butter or margarine	8 eggs
1/4 cup chopped onion	1/4 cup milk
1/4 cup chopped green pepper	1 teaspoon salt
1 (8-oz.) can sauerkraut, drained, rinsed	1/4 teaspoon pepper
1 cup corned beef strips	4 tablespoons butter or margarine
1/4 cup Thousand Island dressing	1 cup shredded Swiss cheese (4 oz.)

Melt 2 tablespoons butter or margarine in a medium skillet. Add onion and green pepper. Cook over medium-high heat until tender, stirring occasionally. Stir in sauerkraut, corned beef and Thousand Island dressing; mix well. Cook until heated through, stirring occasionally. Cover and keep warm over low heat while preparing omelets. In a medium bowl, combine eggs, milk, salt and pepper. Beat with a fork or whisk until mixed well but not frothy. In an 8-inch omelet pan or skillet, melt 1 tablespoon butter or margarine over medium-high heat. When a drop of water sizzles in the pan, pour in 1/4 of the egg mixture. Cook, gently lifting edges so uncooked portion flows underneath, until eggs are set. Spoon about 1/2 cup corned beef mixture onto omelet. Fold omelet and place on a plate. Sprinkle with 1/4 cup cheese. Serve immediately. Repeat with remaining butter or margarine, egg mixture, corned beef mixture and cheese to make 3 more omelets. Makes 4 servings.

Gazpacho Omelet

Classic Spanish soup adds an exotic touch to eggs.

1 tablespoon butter or margarine	2 tablespoons water
1/4 cup chopped cucumber	1/2 teaspoon salt
1/4 cup chopped tomato	1/8 teaspoon pepper
2 tablespoons chopped onion	Dash hot pepper sauce
2 tablespoons chopped green pepper	2 tablespoons butter or margarine
4 eggs	1/2 cup shredded Cheddar cheese (2 oz.)

In an 8-inch omelet pan or skillet, melt 1 tablespoon butter or margarine. Add cucumber, tomato, onion and green pepper. Cook over medium-high heat until onion and pepper are tender, stirring occasionally. Keep warm while preparing omelets. In a small bowl, combine eggs, water, salt, pepper and hot pepper sauce. Beat with a fork or whisk until mixed well but not frothy. In the same omelet pan or skillet, melt 1 tablespoon butter or margarine over medium-high heat. When a drop of water sizzles in the pan, pour in half the egg mixture. Cook, gently lifting edges so uncooked portion flows underneath, until eggs are set. Spoon half the vegetable mixture onto omelet. Fold omelet and place on a plate. Top with 1/4 cup cheese. Serve immediately. Repeat with remaining butter or margarine, egg mixture, vegetable mixture and cheese. Makes 2 servings.

Glorified Omelet

Reminiscent of rice pudding—this omelet will satisfy your sweet tooth.

1 cup cooked rice	1/4 cup milk
1/2 cup sliced banana	1 teaspoon salt
1/2 cup miniature marshmallows	1/4 teaspoon pepper
1 to 2 teaspoons lemon juice	4 tablespoons butter or margarine
1/2 cup pineapple preserves	Pineapple preserves
8 eggs	Chopped pecans

In a medium bowl, mix rice, banana and marshmallows. Sprinkle with lemon juice. Fold in 1/2 cup pineapple preserves; set aside. In another medium bowl, combine eggs, milk, salt and pepper. Beat with a fork or whisk until mixed well but not frothy. In an 8-inch omelet pan or skillet, melt 1 tablespoon butter or margarine over medium-high heat. When a drop of water sizzles in the pan, pour in 1/4 of the egg mixture. Cook, gently lifting edges so uncooked portion flows underneath, until eggs are set. Spoon about 1/2 cup of the rice mixture onto omelet. Fold omelet and place on a plate. Garnish with additional pineapple preserves and chopped pecans. Serve immediately. Repeat with remaining butter or margarine, egg mixture and rice mixture to make 3 more omelets. Makes 4 servings.

Basic Pastry

Packaged pie crust mix can be substituted for this Basic Pastry recipe.

1-1/3 cups all-purpose flour	1/2 cup shortening
1/2 teaspoon salt	3 to 4 tablespoons cold water

In a medium bowl, mix flour and salt. Cut in shortening with a pastry blender or 2 knives until dough resembles coarse peas. Add cold water 1 tablespoon at a time until flour is moistened. Shape dough into a ball. On a lightly floured board, flatten ball into a circle. Roll out dough until it is about 2 inches larger than an inverted 9 or 10-inch pie plate or 3 inches larger than an inverted quiche pan. Fit dough into the pie plate or quiche pan. Trim edges; fold under and flute. For a quiche shell, follow baking instructions found in each recipe. For a baked pastry shell, preheat oven to 450°F (230°C), prick pastry shell thoroughly with a fork, and bake 10 to 12 minutes or until lightly browned. Makes pastry for one 9- or 10-inch pie or quiche.

Party Puffs

These are really easy and you can vary the filling—try the filling for Sausage Soufflé Roll, page 59.

2 tablespoons butter or margarine	6 eggs, separated
2 cups sliced fresh mushrooms	3/4 teaspoon cream of tartar
3 tablespoons chopped shallots or green onions	3 tablespoons all-purpose flour
	1/4 teaspoon salt
2 tablespoons snipped parsley	Dash pepper
1 teaspoon fines herbes	Grated Parmesan cheese
Dash garlic salt	4 to 6 tablespoons butter or margarine

Preheat oven to 325°F (165°C). In a medium skillet, melt 2 tablespoons butter or margarine. Add mushrooms, shallots or green onions, parsley, fines herbes and garlic salt. Cook over medium heat until mushrooms are tender; drain, if necessary. Butter two baking sheets. In a large bowl, beat egg whites and cream of tartar with electric mixer on high speed until stiff peaks form. In a small bowl, beat egg yolks, flour, salt and pepper until thickened and lemon-colored, about 5 minutes. Gently fold yolk mixture into egg whites. In an 8-inch omelet pan or skillet, melt 1 tablespoon butter or margarine over medium heat. When a drop of water sizzles in the pan, spoon 1/2 cup egg mixture into hot butter, spreading to a 5-inch circle. Place 2 tablespoons mushroom mixture on omelet. Sprinkle with Parmesan cheese. Cover with about 1/4 cup egg mixture. Sprinkle again with Parmesan cheese. Cook until puff is slightly set around bottom edge and underside is brown. With a large spatula, place on buttered baking sheet. Add 1/2 to 1 tablespoon butter or margarine to pan and repeat to make 5 more omelets. Place baking sheets in oven. Bake 8 to 10 minutes or until a knife inserted in center of a puff comes out clean. Makes 6 servings.

Cheese Soufflé

Any process cheese can be used in place of the American cheese.

4 tablespoons butter or margarine	1 cup milk
1/4 cup all-purpose flour	1-1/2 cups shredded sharp process American cheese (6 oz.)
1/2 teaspoon salt	
Dash pepper	4 eggs, separated

Preheat oven to 300°F (150°C). In a small saucepan, melt butter or margarine. Blend in flour, salt and pepper. Add milk. Stir constantly over medium-high heat until mixture thickens and bubbles. Remove from heat and add cheese. Stir until cheese is melted. In a large bowl, beat egg whites with electric mixer on high speed until stiff peaks form. In a small bowl, beat egg yolks with electric mixer on high speed until thickened and lemon-colored, about 5 minutes. Gradually stir cheese mixture into egg yolks. Slowly pour egg yolk mixture over egg whites and fold together gently. Pour mixture into an ungreased 1-1/2-quart soufflé dish. Bake 1-1/4 hours or until a knife inserted off-center comes out clean. Serve immediately. Makes 4 to 6 servings.

Oriental Soufflé Pie

Chinese vegetables with a puffy soufflé topper. Sweet & Sour Sauce is the finishing touch.

Basic Pastry, page 57
1/4 cup butter or margarine
1/4 cup all-purpose flour
1/4 teaspoon salt
Dash pepper
1 cup milk
1 (16-oz.) can fancy mixed Chinese
   vegetables, drained well, snipped
2 cups torn fresh spinach

1 (8-oz.) can water chestnuts,
   drained, chopped
1/4 cup chopped green onion
1/4 cup sesame oil
4 eggs, separated
1/2 teaspoon cream of tartar
2 tablespoons sesame seeds, toasted
Sweet & Sour Sauce, below

Preheat oven to 400°F (205°C). Prepare Basic Pastry dough. On a lightly floured board, roll out dough until it is about 2 inches larger than an inverted 10-inch *deep-dish* pie plate. Fit dough into the pie plate. Trim pastry to extend 1/2 to 1 inch beyond edge of pie plate, fold under and flute; do not prick pastry shell. Bake 10 minutes or until lightly browned. Remove from oven. Reduce oven temperature to 300°F (150°C). In a medium saucepan, melt butter or margarine. Blend in flour, salt and pepper. Stir in milk. Stir constantly over medium-high heat until mixture thickens and bubbles. Remove from heat; set aside. In a large skillet, cook Chinese vegetables, spinach, water chestnuts and green onion in sesame oil until spinach is just limp. Drain, if necessary; set aside. In a large bowl, beat egg whites and cream of tartar with electric mixer on high speed until stiff peaks form. In a small bowl, beat egg yolks with electric mixer on high speed until thickened and lemon-colored, about 5 minutes. Gradually beat white sauce mixture into egg yolks. Stir in sesame seeds. Pour egg yolk mixture over beaten egg whites and fold together gently. Spoon vegetables into bottom of pastry shell. Pour soufflé mixture over vegetables. Bake 45 to 55 minutes or until a knife inserted in center comes out clean. Serve immediately with Sweet & Sour Sauce. Makes 8 servings.

Sweet & Sour Sauce

Great flavor! Add cooked chicken, pork or shrimp to any leftover sauce; heat and serve on rice.

1 (8-oz.) can pineapple chunks
1 (8-oz.) can tomato sauce
1/2 cup brown sugar, firmly packed
1/2 cup red wine vinegar

1/2 cup chopped onion
1/2 cup chopped green pepper
2 tablespoons cornstarch
2 tablespoons cold water

Drain pineapple, reserving 1/3 cup juice. Halve pineapple chunks. In a medium saucepan, combine tomato sauce, reserved pineapple juice, brown sugar, vinegar, onion and green pepper. Stir over medium-high heat until mixture boils. Reduce heat. Simmer uncovered 5 minutes. In a small bowl, combine cornstarch and cold water. Stir cornstarch mixture and pineapple into tomato sauce mixture. Stir over medium-high heat until mixture thickens and bubbles. Makes 3 cups of sauce.

California Soufflé Pie

A spectacular entrée! The soufflé top-hat stays perfect longer than you'd expect.

Basic Pastry, page 57
1/4 cup butter or margarine
1/4 cup all-purpose flour
1 teaspoon dillweed
1/4 teaspoon salt
Dash pepper
1 cup milk
1-1/2 cups shredded process Monterey
   Jack cheese (6 oz.)

2 (14-oz.) cans artichoke hearts,
   drained, quartered
1/4 cup chopped pimiento
1/4 cup sliced green onion
1 tablespoon butter or margarine
4 eggs, separated
1/2 teaspoon cream of tartar
Chicken Parmesan Sauce, below
Paprika

Preheat oven to 400°F (205°C). Prepare Basic Pastry dough. On a lightly floured board, roll out dough until it is about 2 inches larger than an inverted 10-inch *deep-dish* pie plate. Fit dough into the pie plate. Trim to extend 1/2 to 1 inch beyond edge of pie plate, fold under and flute; do not prick the pastry shell. Bake 10 minutes or until lightly browned. Remove from oven; set aside. Reduce oven temperature to 300°F (150°C). In a medium saucepan, melt 1/4 cup butter or margarine. Blend in flour, dillweed, salt and pepper. Stir in milk. Stir constantly over medium-high heat until mixture thickens and bubbles. Remove from heat. Add cheese; stir mixture until cheese is melted; set aside. In a medium skillet, cook artichoke hearts, pimiento and green onion in 1 tablespoon butter or margarine until onion is tender. Drain, if necessary; set aside. In a large bowl, beat egg whites and cream of tartar with electric mixer on high speed until stiff peaks form. In a small bowl, beat egg yolks with electric mixer on high speed until thickened and lemon-colored, about 5 minutes. Gradually beat cheese mixture into egg yolks. Pour egg yolk mixture over beaten egg whites and fold together gently. Spoon artichoke mixture into bottom of pastry shell. Pour soufflé mixture over artichoke mixture. Bake 45 to 55 minutes or until a knife inserted in center comes out clean. Serve at once with Chicken Parmesan Sauce, letting guests sprinkle on their own paprika to taste. Makes 8 servings.

Chicken Parmesan Sauce

So good, you can serve it in patty shells or over toast as Chicken a la King.

3 tablespoons butter or margarine
3 tablespoons chopped green onion
2 tablespoons diced pimiento
3 tablespoons all-purpose flour
1/4 teaspoon salt

Dash pepper
3/4 cup milk
1 cup chicken broth
1-1/2 cups cubed cooked chicken
1/4 cup grated Parmesan cheese

In a medium saucepan, melt butter or margarine. Add onion and pimiento. Cook until onion is tender. Blend in flour, salt and pepper. Stir in milk and chicken broth. Stir constantly over medium-high heat until mixture thickens and bubbles. Stir in chicken and Parmesan cheese; heat through. Makes 2-3/4 cups of sauce.

Crab Soufflé Amandine

Amandine *means that almonds are used as an ingredient or garnish.*

6 tablespoons butter or margarine
1/4 cup chopped shallots or green onions
6 tablespoons all-purpose flour
1/2 teaspoon salt
1/8 teaspoon pepper
1-1/2 cups milk
1 (4-oz.) container semisoft natural
   cheese with pepper

1 (7-oz.) can crabmeat, drained,
   flaked, cartilage removed
1 (6-oz.) can sliced mushrooms, drained
6 eggs, separated
3/4 teaspoon cream of tartar
Amandine Sauce, see below

Amandine Sauce:
3 tablespoons butter or margarine
1/4 cup chopped shallots or green onions
2 tablespoons cornstarch
1/4 teaspoon salt
Dash pepper

1-1/2 cups chicken broth
1 tablespoon lemon juice
1/2 cup slivered blanched almonds, toasted,
   page 141
1/4 cup snipped parsley

Preheat oven to 300°F (150°C). In a medium saucepan, melt butter or margarine. Add shallots or green onions. Cook until tender. Blend in flour, salt and pepper. Add milk. Stir constantly over medium-high heat until mixture thickens and bubbles. Remove from heat. Add cheese and stir until melted. Stir in crabmeat and mushrooms. In a large bowl, beat egg whites and cream of tartar with electric mixer on high speed until stiff peaks form. In a small bowl, beat egg yolks with electric mixer on high speed until thickened and lemon-colored, about 5 minutes. Fold crabmeat mixture into egg yolks. Pour egg yolk mixture over beaten egg whites and fold together gently. Pour mixture into an ungreased 2-1/2-quart soufflé dish. Bake 1-1/4 hours or until a knife inserted off-center comes out clean. While soufflé is baking, prepare Amandine Sauce. Serve soufflé immediately with Amandine Sauce. Makes 6 servings.

Amandine Sauce:
In medium saucepan, melt butter or margarine. Add shallots or green onions. Cook until tender. Blend in cornstarch, salt and pepper. Add broth. Stir constantly over medium-high heat until mixture thickens and bubbles. Stir in lemon juice, almonds and parsley. Makes 2 cups of sauce.

Sausage Soufflé Roll

A jelly-roll type soufflé with a spicy sausage and sour cream filling.

Cheese Soufflé mixture, page 58
12 oz. bulk pork sausage
1/2 cup sliced fresh mushrooms

1/4 cup chopped onion
1/4 cup chopped green pepper
1/2 cup dairy sour cream

Preheat oven to 350°F (175°C). Grease a 15" x 10" jelly-roll pan. Line bottom and sides of pan with waxed paper, then grease waxed paper. Prepare mixture for Cheese Soufflé. Pour into prepared jelly-roll pan. Bake 25 minutes or until soufflé is puffed and browned. While soufflé is cooking, combine sausage, mushrooms, onion and green pepper in a medium skillet. Cook over medium heat until sausage is done and vegetables are tender. Drain; place sausage-vegetable mixture in a medium bowl. Stir in sour cream. Place a piece of foil larger than the soufflé on a flat surface. When the soufflé is done, turn out of pan onto foil. Remove waxed paper. Spread sausage filling on soufflé. Lift foil from the short end and roll up soufflé. Slice and serve immediately. Makes 4 to 5 servings.

How To Make Crab Soufflé Amandine

1/Egg whites are critical to a soufflé. Beat the egg whites until peaks stand straight up. Stiffly beaten egg whites will hold a trough when a spatula is drawn through them.

2/To make a top hat on a soufflé, use a knife to make a 1-inch deep circle about 1 inch from edge of the soufflé. Brown-skinned shallots are in the dish behind the foil container of semisoft natural cheese with pepper.

Salmon Rarebit Soufflé

Easy to make—thanks to frozen Welsh rarebit.

1 (10-oz.) pkg. frozen Welsh rarebit, thawed
2 tablespoons all-purpose flour
1 (16-oz.) can salmon, drained, flaked,
  bones removed

1/4 cup snipped parsley
4 eggs, separated
1/2 teaspoon cream of tartar
Yogurt Tartar Sauce, see below

Yogurt Tartar Sauce:
1/2 cup plain yogurt
1/4 cup mayonnaise or salad dressing
1/4 cup chopped dill pickle
3 tablespoons chopped stuffed green olives

Dash salt
Dash pepper
2 Hard-Cooked Eggs, chopped, page 74
2 tablespoons snipped watercress, if desired

Preheat oven to 300°F (150°C). In a medium saucepan, combine a spoonful of rarebit with the flour. Add remaining rarebit. Stir constantly over medium-high heat until bubbly. Remove from heat and stir in salmon and parsley. In a large bowl, beat egg whites and cream of tartar with electric mixer on high speed until stiff peaks form. In a small bowl, beat egg yolks with electric mixer on high speed until thickened and lemon-colored, about 5 minutes. Stir salmon mixture into egg yolks. Pour egg yolk mixture over beaten egg whites and fold together gently. Pour mixture into an ungreased 1-1/2-quart soufflé dish. Bake 1-1/4 hours or until a knife inserted off-center comes out clean. While soufflé is baking, prepare Yogurt Tartar Sauce. Serve soufflé immediately with Yogurt Tartar Sauce. Makes 4 to 6 servings.

Yogurt Tartar Sauce:
In medium bowl, combine yogurt, mayonnaise or salad dressing, dill pickle, olives, salt and pepper. Fold in hard-cooked eggs and watercress, if desired. Chill. Makes 1-1/2 cups of sauce.

Ham & Broccoli Soufflé

You can grind leftover ham or order ground ham from your butcher.

4 tablespoons butter or margarine
1/4 cup all-purpose flour
Dash pepper
1 cup milk
1 cup ground cooked ham

1 (10-oz.) pkg. frozen chopped broccoli,
  thawed, drained
3 tablespoons finely chopped green onion
4 eggs, separated

Preheat oven to 300°F (150°C). In a medium saucepan, melt butter or margarine. Blend in flour and pepper. Add milk. Stir constantly over medium-high heat until mixture thickens and bubbles. Remove from heat and stir in ham, broccoli and green onion. In a large bowl, beat egg whites with electric mixer on high speed until stiff peaks form. In a small bowl, beat egg yolks with electric mixer on high speed until thickened and lemon-colored, about 5 minutes. Stir ham mixture slowly into egg yolks. Gradually pour yolk mixture over egg whites and fold together gently. Pour mixture into an ungreased 1-1/2 quart soufflé dish. Bake 1-1/4 hours or until a knife inserted off-center comes out clean. Serve immediately. Makes 4 to 6 servings.

Eggs & Cheese

Eggs and cheese go together naturally in many dishes, so here they are in recipes that use them separately or together.

Eggs are a very good protein source at relatively low cost. Buy Grade A eggs when appearance is important, as it is in poached eggs. Grade B eggs are fine for baking or scrambling. Medium eggs are a good buy only when they are 7 cents cheaper per dozen than large eggs.

Store eggs in the refrigerator with the large ends up. It is easier to separate eggs when they are cold. Egg whites at room temperature beat up to a larger volume than cold eggs; so let egg whites come to room temperature before beating them.

In general, use low to moderate heat when cooking eggs. French omelets are the exception and they need a hot skillet. The hotter the skillet, the faster the omelet will cook. Adjust the heat according to your ability to keep up with the cooking, filling and folding.

Cheese does wonderful things for baked or scrambled eggs and turns many casseroles into culinary triumphs. Adding a small amount of cheese increases both the flavor and nutrition of any dish.

Be extremely careful when cooking with natural cheeses. They are quite sensitive to high temperatures and have a tendency to become stringy and to separate when overcooked. Well-aged or process cheeses are easier to cook with and give best results in the finished dish.

If you don't have metal steak plates, buy or borrow them so you can make Raclette, page 11.

Arrange a picture-pretty tray of cheese and fruit for dessert. Soft cheeses to enjoy with fruit are Camembert or Brie. Port du Salut or Roquefort are semisoft, and Cheddar, Gruyère, Fontina, Gouda or Edam are from the firm cheese group. Include both crisp fruit such as apples or pears and a more juicy fruit such as grapes, peach wedges or dark sweet cherries. Offer a sweet, full-bodied dessert wine with the cheese and fruit. Red or white port, sweet or cream sherry, muscatel or Tokay are good choices. Sparkling Catawba grape juice is a non-alcoholic beverage to serve with cheese and fruit.

Mexican Egg Cups

Children enjoy eating these little pies they can hold in their hands.

1 (11-oz.) pkg. refrigerated buttermilk
  biscuits (10 biscuits)
1 cup shredded Monterey Jack cheese (4 oz.)
9 eggs, slightly beaten
1/3 cup milk
1/2 cup chopped onion

1/2 cup chopped green pepper
1/3 cup chopped pimiento
1/2 teaspoon salt
1/4 teaspoon hot pepper sauce
5 green olives, halved
Cayenne pepper

Preheat oven to 375°F (190°C). On a lightly floured board, roll out each biscuit to a 5-1/2-inch circle. Pat circles into 10 custard cups so dough comes just to top of cups. Sprinkle 1 tablespoon cheese into each cup; reserve remaining cheese. In a medium bowl, mix eggs, milk, onion, green pepper, pimiento, salt and hot pepper sauce with a fork or whisk. Pour about 1/4 cup of the egg mixture over cheese in each cup. Bake 25 minutes or until a wooden pick inserted in center comes out clean. Sprinkle about 1/2 tablespoon cheese on each egg cup. Top with an olive half. Bake 1 minute or until cheese melts. Sprinkle with cayenne pepper. Makes 5 large or 10 small servings.

Danish Smørrebrød

Decorate this hot open-face sandwich with your favorite garnishes.

4 slices Danish boiled ham
1 (3-oz.) pkg. cream cheese, softened
1 teaspoon prepared horseradish
1 teaspoon prepared mustard
12 slices thinly sliced sour dark rye bread or
   pumpernickel bread, toasted
About 1/4 cup butter or margarine, softened
12 eggs

1/2 teaspoon salt
1/4 teaspoon pepper
1 tablespoon butter or margarine
1 cup sour cream dip with chives
Garnishes such as avocado slices, red caviar,
   tomato wedges and sardines, cooked
   shrimp with capers, parsley sprigs, dill
   sprigs and watercress

Place ham slices on a flat surface. In a small bowl, beat cream cheese, horseradish and mustard with electric mixer on high speed until smooth. Spread cream cheese mixture on ham slices. Roll up tightly starting from short end. Wrap and chill. Slice thinly before scrambling eggs. Preheat oven to 200°F (95°C). Butter toast generously with butter and keep warm in oven. In a large bowl, beat eggs, salt and pepper with fork or whisk until frothy. In a large skillet, melt 1 tablespoon butter or margarine over medium heat. Add egg mixture. Scramble eggs by lifting edges so uncooked portion flows underneath. When eggs are just set, stir in 1/2 cup sour cream dip. Remove toast from oven and place on plates. Spoon egg mixture on top of toast. Garnish as shown in the photograph or as desired. Makes 6 servings.

Creamy Egg Croquettes

A crisp outer-coating and a creamy filling.

1-1/2 tablespoons butter or margarine
3 tablespoons all-purpose flour
1/8 teaspoon salt
1/2 cup milk
6 Hard-Cooked Eggs, page 74,
   very finely chopped or ground
2 tablespoons chopped pimiento
2 tablespoons chopped green onion

2 teaspoons snipped chives
1/2 teaspoon salt
1/4 teaspoon dry mustard
2 eggs, slightly beaten
2 tablespoons milk
Vegetable oil for deep frying
1 cup fine dry breadcrumbs

In a small saucepan, melt butter or margarine. Blend in flour and 1/8 teaspoon salt. Add 1/2 cup milk. Stir constantly over medium-high heat until mixture thickens and bubbles. Remove from heat and cool thoroughly. Prepare Hard-Cooked Eggs. In a medium bowl, mix cooled sauce, Hard-Cooked Eggs, pimiento, green onion, chives, 1/2 teaspoon salt and dry mustard. Cover and refrigerate mixture at least 4 hours. Shape into 8 croquettes, using about 1/4 cup mixture for each. In a pie plate, mix slightly beaten eggs and 2 tablespoons milk. Heat oil in a deep heavy pot to 365°F (185°C); at this temperature a 1-inch cube of bread dropped into oil will turn golden brown in 50 to 60 seconds. Roll croquettes in breadcrumbs, then in egg mixture, then in breadcrumbs again. Fry in deep hot oil 1-1/2 to 2 minutes or until browned. Drain on paper towels. Serve immediately or keep warm in preheated oven (200°F, 95°C). Makes 8 servings.

Western Frittata

Italian omelet in a skillet. Chock full of vegetables and robustly seasoned.

4 slices bacon
1 cup chopped zucchini
1/3 cup chopped green pepper
1/3 cup chopped onion
1-1/4 cups cooked small shell macaroni,
    drained (1/2 cup uncooked)

1/2 teaspoon celery salt
1/2 to 1 teaspoon dried oregano, crushed
1/4 teaspoon pepper
6 eggs, beaten
1/4 cup grated Romano cheese
Dairy sour cream or chili sauce

In an 8-inch oven-proof skillet, cook bacon until crisp. Drain on paper towels. Reserve 2 table-spoons drippings in skillet. Crumble bacon and set aside. Cook zucchini, green pepper and onion in reserved bacon drippings until tender. Stir in cooked macaroni, celery salt, oregano, pepper and bacon. Preheat broiler at moderate temperature. Pour eggs evenly over zucchini mixture in skillet. Cook over medium heat until bottom is set and slightly browned, about 5 minutes. Place under preheated broiler about 3 inches from the heat; broil 2 minutes. Sprinkle with Romano cheese. Broil 1 to 2 minutes more or until top is set and lightly browned. Set in wedges topped with sour cream or chili sauce. Makes 4 to 6 servings.

German Farmer's Breakfast

Covered with chunks of potato and bratwurst, these eggs are not for dainty appetites.

6 slices bacon
1/4 cup chopped green onion
1/4 cup chopped green pepper
1 tablespoon all-purpose flour
1 tablespoon sugar
1/2 teaspoon celery seeds
1/4 teaspoon salt
Dash pepper
1/2 cup water
1/4 cup vinegar
2 cups cubed cooked potatoes or 1 (16-oz.)
    can whole new potatoes, drained, cubed

8 oz. fully cooked smoked bratwurst,
    cut in 1/2-inch pieces (about 2 cups)
1/4 cup chopped pimiento
2 tablespoons butter or margarine
8 eggs, beaten
1/3 cup milk
1/2 teaspoon salt
Dash pepper
Snipped parsley, if desired

In a large skillet, cook bacon until crisp. Remove bacon from skillet. Drain on paper towels. Reserve 3 tablespoons drippings in skillet. Crumble bacon and set aside. Cook green onion and green pepper in reserved drippings until tender. Blend in flour, sugar, celery seeds, 1/4 teaspoon salt and dash pepper. Stir in water and vinegar. Stir constantly over medium-high heat until mixture thickens and bubbles. Fold in potatoes, bratwurst and pimiento. Heat until bubbly. Reduce heat and keep hot while scrambling eggs. In a large skillet, melt butter or margarine over medium heat. Mix eggs with milk, 1/2 teaspoon salt and dash pepper. Add to skillet. Cook over medium heat, lifting edges of egg mixture so uncooked portion flows underneath. When eggs are cooked throughout but still glossy and moist, remove from skillet and place on a heated platter. Top with hot potato mixture. Garnish with crumbled bacon and snipped parsley, if desired. Makes 6 to 8 servings.

Smoky Egg Casserole

The best scrambled eggs you ever ate, and you made them the night before!

2 tablespoons butter or margarine
2 tablespoons all-purpose flour
1-1/4 cups milk
1 (6-oz.) roll smoke-flavored cheese spread
6 slices bacon
3 slices bread, cut in 1/4-inch cubes
12 eggs, slightly beaten

1 cup frozen peas, cooked, drained
1 (6-oz.) can sliced mushrooms, drained
1/2 cup chopped pimiento
2 tablespoons snipped chives
1 tablespoon vegetable oil
1 tomato, cut in wedges
Snipped chives

In a medium saucepan, melt butter or margarine. Blend in flour. Add milk. Stir constantly over medium-high heat until mixture thickens and bubbles. Reduce heat to low. Stir in cheese spread until melted; set aside. In a large skillet, cook bacon over medium-high heat until crisp. Drain on paper towels. Reserve drippings in skillet. Crumble bacon and refrigerate. To make croutons, cook bread cubes in bacon drippings until crisp, stirring occasionally. Remove croutons and set aside. In a medium bowl, mix eggs, peas, mushrooms, pimiento and 2 tablespoons chives. In the same large skillet, heat oil. Add egg mixture. Cook over medium-high heat, gently lifting edges of egg mixture so uncooked portion flows underneath. When eggs are set, fold in cheese spread mixture. Turn mixture into a 12" x 7" baking dish. Cover and refrigerate overnight. About 30 minutes before serving, preheat oven to 350°F (175°C). Remove cover from casserole. Bake 20 minutes. Top with croutons and crumbled bacon. Bake 10 minutes or until heated through. Garnish with tomato wedges and snipped chives. Makes 6 to 8 servings.

Huevos Rancheros

Start off your Mexican brunch with a pitcher of Tequila Sunrise, page 29.

2 tablespoons vegetable oil
4 (6-inch) corn tortillas
1/2 cup chopped onion
1 garlic clove, minced
1 (28-oz.) can tomatoes, drained, cut up
1 (4-oz.) can whole green chilies,
   drained, seeded, chopped

1 tablespoon cornstarch
1 tablespoon cold water
1/2 teaspoon cumin
4 eggs
3/4 cup shredded Cheddar cheese (3 oz.)

Preheat oven to 350°F (175°C). Heat oil in a medium skillet. Fry tortillas 1 at a time 20 seconds or until heated through but not crisp, turning once. Cut tortillas in half; set aside. In the same skillet, cook onion and garlic over medium-high heat until onion is tender. Add tomatoes and green chilies; bring to a boil. Reduce heat and simmer uncovered 15 minutes to blend flavors. In a small bowl, combine cornstarch, water and cumin. Stir into tomato mixture. Stir constantly over medium-high heat until mixture thickens and bubbles. Pour into an 8-inch square baking dish. Stand tortilla halves around inside edge of baking dish. Make 4 wells in tomato mixture. Break eggs into wells. Bake about 20 minutes or until eggs are set. Sprinkle with cheese. Bake 1 minute longer or until cheese melts. Makes 4 servings.

Tortilla Español

In Spain, a tortilla is a omelet. Decrease the chilies if you prefer yours less picante.

3 tablespoons olive oil
1 small leek, thinly sliced (1/2 to 3/4 cup)
1 garlic clove, minced
1/4 cup sliced pitted black olives
1 (4-oz.) can whole green chilies, drained, seeded, chopped
1 (16-oz.) can sliced potatoes, drained
6 eggs

1/2 teaspoon dried thyme
1/2 teaspoon salt
1/8 teaspoon pepper
2 tablespoons snipped parsley
2 tomatoes, cut in wedges
Olive oil
Dash salt
Dash pepper

In a 10-inch oven-proof skillet, heat 3 tablespoons olive oil. Add leeks and garlic. Cook until leeks are tender. Stir in olives and chilies. Gently stir in potatotes. Arrange evenly over bottom of skillet. Heat through. In a medium bowl, combine eggs, thyme, 1/2 teaspoon salt and 1/8 teaspoon pepper. Beat with a fork or whisk until mixed well but not frothy. Stir in parsley. Pour over vegetable mixture in skillet. Cook over medium heat until tortilla is lightly browned on bottom, 8 to 10 minutes. While tortilla is cooking, brush tomato wedges with olive oil. Sprinkle with salt and pepper. Preheat broiler at moderate temperature. Place tortilla in skillet and tomato wedges on a baking sheet in preheated broiler 3 inches from the heat. Broil until tortilla is set and browned, 4 to 5 minutes. Remove from broiler; let tortilla stand a minute or two. Cut in wedges. Top with tomato wedges. Serve immediately. Makes 6 servings.

How To Make Scotch Eggs

1/Shape the sausage mixture into 6 patties. Place a hard-cooked egg in the center of each patty. Mold the patty around the egg, completely covering the egg.

2/Chill the sausage-wrapped eggs, then dip in flour, beaten egg, and finally breadcrumbs. Cook in hot deep oil until golden brown. Serve either warm or chilled with Creamy Horseradish Sauce.

Breakfast Salad

Artichoke hearts in a hot cream sauce are poured over soft poached eggs and salad greens.

3 tablespoons butter or margarine
3 slices white bread, crusts removed,
   cut in 1/2-inch cubes
Dash garlic salt
1/2 teaspoon dried tarragon, crushed
1 cup diced Canadian bacon or ham
2 tablespoons chopped green onion
4 tablespoons butter or margarine
1 tablespoon all-purpose flour

1 tablespoon sugar
1/2 teaspoon salt
1/4 teaspoon pepper
2/3 cup water
1/4 cup tarragon vinegar
1 (14-oz.) can artichoke hearts, drained,
   quartered
6 cups torn mixed greens
6 soft Poached Eggs page 73

In a large skillet, melt 3 tablespoons butter or margarine. Add bread cubes, garlic salt and tarragon. Toss over medium-high heat until bread cubes are toasted. Remove croutons from skillet and set aside. In the same skillet, cook Canadian bacon and green onion in 4 tablespoons butter or margarine until onion is tender. Stir in flour, sugar, salt and pepper. Add water and vinegar. Stir over medium-high heat until mixture thickens and bubbles. Reduce heat. Add artichoke hearts; heat through. Place crisp greens on 6 salad plates. Place a poached egg on greens on each plate. Spoon hot sauce mixture over eggs and greens. Top with croutons. Makes 6 servings.

Scotch Eggs

Hard-cooked eggs are wrapped in a spicy sausage coating and deep fried.

6 Hard-Cooked Eggs, peeled, page 74
Creamy Horseradish Sauce, see below
12 oz. bulk pork sausage
2 tablespoons snipped parsley
1/2 teaspoon rubbed sage
1/2 teaspoon dried thyme

1/4 cup all-purpose flour
1/8 teaspoon salt
Dash pepper
Vegetable oil for deep-frying
1 egg, slightly beaten
1/2 cup fine dry breadcrumbs, page 77

Creamy Horseradish Sauce:
3/4 cup dairy sour cream
3 tablespoons prepared horseradish

1 tablespoon prepared mustard

Prepare Hard-Cooked Eggs. Prepare Creamy Horseradish Sauce and refrigerate. In a medium bowl, mix sausage, parsley, sage and thyme. Shape sausage mixture into six patties about four inches in diameter. Wrap each Hard-Cooked Egg with a sausage patty, covering the egg completely. Cover eggs and refrigerate at least four hours. In a pie plate, mix flour, salt and pepper. Heat oil in a deep heavy pot to 350°F (175°C); at this temperature a 1-inch cube of bread dropped into oil will turn golden brown in 65 seconds. Roll sausage-wrapped eggs in flour mixture, then in beaten egg, then in breadcrumbs. Fry in deep hot oil 2 minutes or until browned. Drain on paper towels. Serve hot or cold with Creamy Horseradish Sauce. Makes 6 servings.

Creamy Horseradish Sauce:
In a small bowl, mix sour cream, horseradish and mustard. Makes 3/4 cup of sauce.

Bacon & Egg Croissants   *Photo on cover.*

Croissants are a delicious, flaky alternative to muffins or toast.

4 croissants, split
3 tablespoons butter or margarine, softened
8 bacon slices
4 Poached Eggs, opposite

Double recipe Cheddar Sauce, page 53
Snipped chives
Chopped pimiento

Preheat broiler at moderate temperature. Spread split side of croissant halves with butter or margarine. Broil 3 to 4 inches from heat until lightly toasted. In a medium skillet, cook bacon until crisp. Drain on paper towels. Place 2 bacon slices on bottom half of each croissant; keep warm. Bring water to a boil for Poached Eggs. While water is heating, prepare double recipe of Cheddar Sauce. Prepare Poached Eggs. Place Poached Eggs on top of bacon slices. Top with Cheddar Sauce. Garnish with snipped chives and chopped pimiento. Serve each egg-topped croissant half with top half on the side. Makes 4 servings.

How To Make Rarebit au Gratin

1/Place a toasted English muffin half in an au gratin dish. Cut another muffin half down the middle and place the pieces, cut edges down, on each side of the muffin half. Top with a grilled tomato slice and 2 strips of crisp bacon.

2/Ladle the cheese sauce over the muffins and sprinkle with Parmesan breadcrumbs before baking.

Poached Eggs

An easy method for perfect poached eggs. Vinegar helps to set the egg whites.

Water	**4 eggs**
1 tablespoon white wine vinegar	**Salt and pepper to taste**

In a 3-quart saucepan, pour water to a depth of 3 inches. Add vinegar and bring to a boil. Reduce heat to keep water just simmering. Break 1 egg into a shallow dish. Stir simmering water to make it swirl. Gently slip egg into swirling water, following swirl. Cook 2 to 3 minutes until egg is set as desired. Remove egg with a slotted spoon. Trim edges, if desired. Season to taste with salt and pepper. Repeat with remaining eggs. Makes 4 servings.

Rarebit au Gratin

Stack bacon and tomato slices on English muffins, then pour a thick cheese sauce over the stacks.

2 tablespoons butter or margarine	**12 slices bacon**
1 cup soft breadcrumbs	**6 thick tomato slices**
1/4 cup grated Parmesan cheese	**6 English muffins, split, buttered, toasted**
1 tablespoon snipped chives	**Rarebit Sauce, see below**
1 teaspoon paprika	

Rarebit Sauce:

1 cup shredded process American cheese	**1 teaspoon dry mustard**
(4 oz.)	**2 teaspoons Worcestershire sauce**
1 cup shredded Swiss cheese (4 oz.)	**2 egg yolks, beaten**
1-1/4 cups half-and-half	

Preheat oven to 350°F (175°C). In a small saucepan, melt butter or margarine. Add breadcrumbs, Parmesan cheese, chives and paprika; toss and set aside. In a large skillet, cook bacon over medium-high heat until crisp. Drain on paper towels. Reserve 3 tablespoons drippings in skillet. Cook tomato slices in reserved drippings until tender. Place 6 of the muffin halves in 6 individual au gratin dishes. Cut remaining 6 muffin halves crosswise and stand 2 pieces cut-side down along edges of each dish. Place a tomato slice and 2 slices of bacon on top of each muffin half. Place au gratin dishes in oven while preparing Rarebit Sauce. Ladle sauce over muffin stacks in au gratin dishes. Top with the breadcrumb mixture. Bake 15 to 20 minutes or until bubbly and browned. Makes 6 servings.

Rarebit Sauce:
In a heavy saucepan, mix American cheese, Swiss cheese, half-and-half, dry mustard and Worcestershire sauce. Stir constantly over low heat, until melted. Stir 1 cup of hot sauce into egg yolks; mix well. Add egg yolk mixture to hot mixture in saucepan. Stir constantly over medium heat until mixture thickens.

Eggs Benedict

Classic Hollandaise Sauce is the topper, but you can use a Hollandaise Sauce mix.

4 English muffins, split	8 Poached Eggs, page 73
3 tablespoons butter or margarine, softened	Hollandaise Sauce, see below
1 tablespoon vegetable oil	4 olives, halved
8 (1/4-inch) slices Canadian bacon (about 12 oz.)	Sliced pimiento

Hollandaise Sauce:

6 egg yolks	2 tablespoons lemon juice
1 cup butter or margarine	Dash white pepper

Preheat broiler at moderate temperature. Spread split side of muffin halves with butter or margarine. Broil 3 to 4 inches from heat until toasted as desired. Heat oil in a large skillet. Add Canadian bacon. Cook over medium-high heat until browned, turning once. Place on English muffins; keep warm. Bring water to a boil for Poached Eggs. While water is heating, prepare Hollandaise Sauce. Prepare Poached Eggs. Place Poached Eggs on top of Canadian bacon slices. Top with Hollandaise Sauce. Place an olive half in the center of each egg. Arrange pimiento slices around olive half to form a pinwheel shape. Makes 6 to 8 servings.

Hollandaise Sauce:
In a small bowl, beat egg yolks with a whisk until slightly thickened; set aside. In a small saucepan, melt butter or margarine. Place egg yolks in the top of a double boiler. Place pan over simmering but not boiling water. Add melted butter or margarine a little at a time while rapidly stirring egg yolks. Stir constantly over low heat until thickened to the consistency of heavy cream, about 10 minutes. Remove from heat. Stir in lemon juice and pepper. Cover to keep warm.

Hard-Cooked Eggs

A fool-proof method for perfect hard-cooked eggs every time!

Water	Salt
6 eggs	

Place eggs in a 2-quart saucepan. Add enough cold water to cover at least 1-inch above eggs. Eggs will be easier to peel if you add 1-1/2 teaspoons salt for each quart of water. Bring water to a boil over high heat. Immediately reduce heat and keep water just below simmering. Cover eggs and cook 20 minutes. Immediately plunge eggs in cold water to prevent yolk darkening. Let stand in cold water to cool. To peel, crack eggs all over and roll on counter top to loosen shell. Peel under running water starting at large end. Air pocket at large end makes it easier to start peeling. Makes 6 servings.

Cheese & Spinach Pie

Look for filo *or* phyllo *in the frozen food section of your supermarket—and pronounce it* fee-low.

2 tablespoons butter or margarine
1/2 cup chopped onion
1/2 cup chopped green pepper
1 (10-oz.) pkg. frozen chopped spinach, thawed
2 tomatoes, peeled, seeded, chopped
2 teaspoons dried oregano, crushed
2 eggs

1 (11-oz.) can condensed Cheddar cheese soup
1 (8-oz.) carton plain yogurt
1/2 cup (2-oz.) crumbled feta cheese
1/4 cup all-purpose flour
8 (16" x 3") frozen filo leaves, thawed
1/2 cup butter or margarine, melted

Preheat oven to 325°F (165°C). Grease a 12" x 7" baking dish; set aside. In a medium skillet, melt 2 tablespoons butter or margarine. Add onion and green pepper. Cook over medium-high heat until tender, stirring occasionally. Squeeze excess water from spinach. Add spinach, tomatoes and oregano to skillet. Remove from heat and set aside. In a medium bowl, beat eggs. Blend in soup, yogurt, feta cheese and flour. Fold spinach mixture into egg mixture. Brush 1 sheet of filo dough with melted butter or margarine. Fold in half to form an 8" x 3" rectangle. Place in greased baking dish. Repeat with 2 more sheets of filo. Spoon spinach mixture over dough in baking dish. Brush remaining sheets of filo with remaining melted butter or margarine. Fold each one in half and place over spinach filling, tucking in edges. Bake 45 to 50 minutes, until filling is set and top is golden brown. Let stand 10 minutes before serving. Cut into squares. Makes 6 servings.

Cheese-Sausage Scramble

Eggs spiced with sausage and laced with melting cheese give the day an energizing start.

9 sausage links, (9 oz.), cut in 1/2-inch pieces
1/2 cup sliced fresh mushrooms
1/4 cup chopped green onion
2 tablespoons chopped pimiento

6 eggs
2 tablespoons milk
Dash pepper
2 oz. Cheddar cheese, cut in 1/4-inch cubes

In a medium skillet, cook sausage pieces over medium heat until browned. Remove sausage, reserving 2 tablespoons drippings in skillet. Cook mushrooms, onions and pimiento in drippings until tender. In a medium bowl, beat eggs, milk and pepper with a fork or whisk until mixed well but not frothy. Add to mushroom mixture in skillet. Cook until eggs are almost set, about 3 minutes, stirring occasionally. Stir in cooked sausage and cheese. Continue cooking and occasionally stirring until eggs are set, about 2 minutes longer. Makes 4 servings.

Variation

Bacon-Onion Scramble: Substitute 6 slices bacon for sausage. Substitute 1/4 cup chopped yellow or white onion for green onion and 1/4 cup chopped green pepper for mushrooms.

Peaches & Cream French Toast

Best with fresh peaches but you can use sliced canned freestone peaches.

3 eggs
3 tablespoons peach preserves
3/4 cup half-and-half
6 slices French bread, cut 1/2 inch thick
1/3 cup peach preserves

1/2 cup butter or margarine, softened
2 fresh peaches, peeled, sliced
Powdered sugar
Toasted almonds, page 141
Powdered sugar

In a small bowl, beat eggs and 3 tablespoons peach preserves with a fork or whisk to blend. Beat in half-and-half. Place a single layer of bread slices in an 11" x 7" baking dish. Pour egg mixture over bread. Cover and refrigerate a few hours or overnight until most of the liquid is absorbed. In a small bowl, beat 1/3 cup peach preserves and 4 tablespoons softened butter or margarine with electric mixer on high speed until fluffy; set aside until ready to serve. At serving time, melt 2 tablespoons butter or margarine in a large skillet. Add 3 bread slices and cook over medium-high heat until browned, turning once. Remove from skillet and keep warm. Repeat with remaining bread slices and butter or margarine. Serve French Toast topped with about 1 tablespoon peach butter and peach slices. Sprinkle with toasted almonds and powdered sugar. Makes 4 to 6 servings.

How To Make Peaches & Cream French Toast

1/A few hours or the night before your brunch, arrange French bread slices in a shallow dish. Pour the egg and cream mixture over the bread slices and refrigerate until the mixture is absorbed.

2/Brown the French bread in melted butter or margarine in a large skillet. Serve with jam-butter mixture, fresh peach slices and toasted almonds. Sprinkle with powdered sugar.

Breads

All the bread recipes in this book use the fool-proof easy method of combining ingredients—your electric mixer does the work. Be sure to try Buttery Croissants which are in the menu on page 19.

To raise yeast dough, place it in a greased bowl, then turn the dough over to grease it on all sides. Cover the bowl and place it on a rack in a cold oven with a large bowl of hot water underneath. Yeast organisms require a warm environment to grow but high temperatures will kill them.

To punch down and knead yeast dough, plunge your fist into the center of the risen dough. Fold the dough over the hole left by your fist and turn it out onto a lightly floured board. Shape it into a ball. Slightly flatten it and fold half the dough toward you. Push the dough away from you with the heels of your palms. This is one knead. Give the dough a quarter turn and repeat folding and pushing until the dough is smooth and elastic.

No time for yeast bread today? Then look through this section for the quick breads.

Grease only the bottoms of muffin pan cups. If the sides of the cups are greased, the batter will rise until it spills over the edge of the cups, giving uneven, unprofessional looking muffins. If the sides of the cups are ungreased, the batter will cling to them and rise only slightly, giving a smooth, nicely rounded top with neat edges.

For perfect muffins, stir batter only a few strokes until the flour mixture is moistened. Then gently ease the batter into pans with a spatula. Over-beating or dropping batter from a spoon may cause a peaked top and an uneven tunneled texture.

To freeze breads, cool them to room temperature on a wire rack. Wrap them in freezer wrap, heavy-duty foil or heavy-weight plastic freezer bags and freeze them. They will keep from 9 to 12 months. To thaw breads, let them stand wrapped at room temperature 2 to 3 hours. Or wrap them loosely in aluminum foil and heat them in a 350°F (175°C) oven for 20 to 25 minutes. Add frosting or other topping after the bread has been thawed.

MAKE YOUR OWN BREADCRUMBS

Tear a slice of bread into several pieces. Whirl them in a blender or food processor. If you don't have a blender or processor, scrape crumbs from the bread slices with a fork. You can season your breadcrumbs with salt, pepper, garlic powder and powdered or crushed dried herbs. From 1 slice of bread you can make 1/2 cup of soft breadcrumbs or 1/4 cup of dry breadcrumbs.

Old Fashioned Buttermilk Biscuits

Friends of ours serve these hot with lots of butter and honey.

2 cups all-purpose flour	1/4 teaspoon baking soda
1 tablespoon baking powder	1/3 cup shortening
2 teaspoons sugar	3/4 cup buttermilk
1 teaspoon salt	

Preheat oven to 450°F (230°C). In a medium bowl, mix flour, baking powder, sugar, salt and baking soda. Cut in shortening with a pastry blender or 2 knives until mixture resembles coarse peas. Add buttermilk to flour mixture. Stir only until dough clings together. On a lightly floured board, knead dough gently with fingertips 25 to 30 times. Gently roll out dough 1/2 inch thick. Cut with a floured 2-1/2-inch biscuit cutter. Bake biscuits on an ungreased baking sheet 15 minutes or until golden brown. Makes 9 biscuits.

Pictured on the following pages. Clockwise from the top right: Caramel-Pecan Sticky Buns, page 87; Lemon-Cheese Stars, page 82; Bubble Bread, page 85; Cinnamon Twist Coffeecake, page 90; Sunny Orange Braid, page 81.

Basic Sweet Dough

Use this dough to create the sweet breads on the following pages.

1/2 cup milk
4 tablespoons butter or margarine
2 tablespoons water
2-3/4 to 3 cups all-purpose flour

1/4 cup sugar
1/2 teaspoon salt
1 pkg. active dry yeast
1 egg

Grease a large bowl; set aside. In a medium saucepan, mix milk, butter or margarine and water. Heat only until warm (120°F, 50°C); the butter does not need to melt. In a large bowl, mix 1 cup flour, sugar, salt and yeast. Add warm milk mixture. Beat with electric mixer on medium speed 2 minutes, scraping bowl occasionally. Add egg and 1/2 cup flour. Beat with electric mixer on high speed 2 minutes, scraping bowl occasionally. By hand, stir in enough of the remaining flour to make a moderately stiff dough. On a lightly floured board, knead dough 3 to 5 minutes or until smooth and elastic. Place in the greased bowl, turning once to grease top. Cover and let rise in a warm place about 1 hour or until doubled in bulk. To test if dough is ready to punch down, press your finger in the center. If the hole made remains and an air bubble forms to the side, it is ready. Punch down; turn out onto a lightly floured board. Cover and let stand 10 minutes. Makes enough dough for 1 recipe Bubble Bread, Sunny Orange Braid, Caramel-Pecan Sticky Buns, Lemon-Cheese Stars or Cinnamon Twist Coffeecake.

Honey-Glazed Bow Knots

Although the knots can be done in a jiffy, the glaze needs an hour to cool.

Honey Glaze, see below
1 (7.5-oz.) pkg. refrigerated biscuits
   (10 biscuits)

2 tablespoons butter or margarine, melted
1/2 cup sugar
1/2 teaspoon ground cinnamon

Honey Glaze:
1/3 cup honey
3 tablespoons water

Prepare Honey Glaze; set aside. Preheat oven to 400°F (205°C). Grease a baking sheet; set aside. On a lightly floured board, roll each biscuit with your hands into a 6-inch rope, stretching gently if necessary. Brush with melted butter or margarine. In a shallow dish or on a sheet of waxed paper, mix sugar and cinnamon. Roll ropes in cinnamon-sugar mixture. Loosely tie each rope into a knot, stretching gently if necessary. Place knots on the greased baking sheet. Bake 10 to 12 minutes or until golden brown. Remove from baking sheet. Cool on rack 10 minutes. Glaze with Honey Glaze. Makes 10 knots.

Honey Glaze:
In a small saucepan, mix honey and water. Cook over medium heat until blended, stirring occasionally. Cool in refrigerator 1 hour.

Sunny Orange Braid *Photo on page 78.*

A delectable bread filled with orange marmalade and crowned with a crumbly topping.

Basic Sweet Dough, page 80
1/2 cup orange marmalade
1/4 cup sliced almonds
3 tablespoons all-purpose flour

1 tablespoon sugar
1 tablespoon grated orange peel
1 tablespoon butter or margarine, melted

Prepare Basic Sweet Dough. Grease a baking sheet. On a lightly floured board, roll out dough to a 13" x 8" rectangle. Place rectangle on the greased baking sheet. In a small bowl, combine orange marmalade and almonds. Spread orange marmalade mixture lengthwise on center third of dough. Along longest sides of dough, make a crosswise cut every inch from filling to edge of dough. Fold strips at an angle across filling, alternating from side to side. In a small bowl, combine flour, sugar and orange peel. Stir in melted butter or margarine until mixture is crumbly. Sprinkle braid with flour mixture. Cover and let rise in a warm place about 30 minutes or until doubled in bulk. Preheat oven to 375°F (190°C). Bake 35 minutes or until golden brown. Remove from baking sheet. Cool on rack. Makes 1 loaf.

How To Make Sunny Orange Braid

1/Roll out dough to a 13" x 8" rectangle. Place on a greased baking sheet. Spread the center third of dough with marmalade mixture. At one-inch intervals, cut the dough from filling to the outside edge. Fold the strips at an angle across dough, alternating from side to side.

2/You can seal the ends of the dough together with a little water, if necessary. Sprinkle the loaf with the crumb topping. Cover and let it rise.

Lemon-Cheese Stars *Photo on page 78.*

Cream cheese flavored with fresh lemon makes a glorious filling.

Basic Sweet Dough, page 80
2 (3-oz.) pkgs. cream cheese, softened
1 egg, separated

3 tablespoons sugar
2 teaspoons lemon juice
1/2 teaspoon grated lemon peel

Prepare Basic Sweet Dough. Grease 2 baking sheets. On a lightly floured board, roll out dough to a 12" x 9" rectangle. Cut rectangle into twelve 3-inch squares. Cut squares diagonally from each corner to about 1/2 inch from center. Place squares on the greased baking sheets about 1 inch apart. In a medium bowl, beat cream cheese, egg yolk, sugar, lemon juice and lemon peel with electric mixer on high speed until light and fluffy. Spoon about 1 tablespoon cream cheese mixture onto center of each square. Bring every other corner to the center of the square; pinch points securely in center to seal. Repeat with remaining squares. Cover and let rise in a warm place about 30 minutes or until doubled in bulk. Preheat oven to 400°F (205°C). In a small bowl, beat egg white with a fork. Brush stars with egg white. Bake 10 minutes or until golden brown. Remove from baking sheets. Cool on rack. Makes 12 stars.

How To Make Lemon-Cheese Stars

1/Roll out dough to a 12″ x 9″ rectangle. Cut the rectangle into twelve squares. Cut the square diagonally from each corner to about 1/2 inch from the square's center.

2/Place squares on a greased baking sheet and spoon cheese filling onto the center of each square. Bring alternate corners of the squares to the center and pinch to seal. Cover and let rise before baking.

Crumb Kuchen

Buttery crumb topping melts into the rich batter while the coffeecake is baking.

1/2 cup milk	1 cup all-purpose flour
1/4 cup water	1/2 cup granulated sugar
1/2 cup butter or margarine	1/2 cup brown sugar, firmly packed
2 cups all-purpose flour	2 teaspoons ground cinnamon
1/4 cup granulated sugar	6 tablespoons butter or margarine
1/4 teaspoon salt	1 egg yolk
1 pkg. active dry yeast	Powdered sugar
1 egg	

Grease a 9-inch square pan. In a medium saucepan, mix milk, water and 1/2 cup butter or margarine. Heat only until warm (120°F, 50°C); butter does not need to melt. In a large bowl, mix 1/2 cup flour, 1/4 cup granulated sugar, salt and yeast. Add warm milk mixture. Beat with electric mixer on medium speed 2 minutes, scraping bowl occasionally. Add 1 cup flour and 1 egg. Beat with electric mixer on high speed 2 minutes, scraping bowl occasionally. By hand, stir in 1/2 cup flour. Spread batter into the greased baking pan. In a medium bowl, mix 1 cup flour, 1/2 cup granulated sugar, brown sugar and cinnamon. With a pastry blender or 2 knives, cut in 6 tablespoons butter or margarine and egg yolk. Crumble brown sugar mixture over top of batter. Cover and let rise in a warm place about 1 hour or until doubled in bulk. Preheat oven to 350°F (175°C). Bake 40 minutes. Sprinkle with powdered sugar. Cool about 30 minutes. Serve slightly warm. Makes 1 coffeecake.

Cheddar Cheese Bread *Photo on page 5.*

For a lightly floured board, use about 1 tablespoon of flour from each cup of flour in the recipe.

1-3/4 cups water	2 pkgs. active dry yeast
1 cup milk	3 cups shredded sharp Cheddar cheese
8 to 8-1/2 cups all-purpose flour	(12-oz.)
1/4 cup sugar	2 tablespoons butter or margarine, melted
1 tablespoon salt	2 tablespoons sesame seeds

Grease a large bowl and two 9" x 5" loaf pans; set aside. In a medium saucepan, mix water and milk. Heat only until warm (120°F, 50°C). In a large bowl, mix 2-1/2 cups flour, sugar, salt and yeast. Add warm milk mixture. Beat with electric mixer on medium speed 2 minutes, scraping bowl occasionally. Add cheese and 1/2 cup flour. Beat with electric mixer on high speed 2 minutes, scraping bowl occasionally. By hand, stir in enough of the remaining flour to make a moderately stiff dough. On a lightly floured board, knead dough about 10 minutes or until smooth and elastic. Place dough in the greased bowl, turning once to grease top. Cover and let rise in a warm place about 1 hour or until doubled in bulk. Punch down; turn onto a lightly floured board. Cover and let stand 15 minutes. Divide dough in half; shape into 2 loaves. Place loaves in greased pans. Cover and let rise in a warm place about 1 hour or until doubled in bulk. Preheat oven to 375°F (190°C). Brush loaves with melted butter or margarine. Sprinkle with sesame seeds. Bake about 40 minutes, until loaves sound hollow when tapped with your finger. Remove loaves from pans; cool on rack. Makes 2 loaves.

Braided Egg Ring

Pop the unbaked loaves into the refrigerator and let them rise overnight.

1-1/2 cups milk	1 tablespoon salt
3/4 cup water	2 pkgs. active dry yeast
4 tablespoons butter or margarine	4 eggs
8-1/2 to 8-3/4 cups all-purpose flour	Vegetable oil
3 tablespoons sugar	

Grease 2 baking sheets; set aside. In a medium saucepan, mix milk, water and butter or margarine. Heat only until warm (120°F, 50°C); the butter does not need to melt. In a large bowl, mix 3 cups flour, sugar, salt and yeast. Add warmed milk mixture. Beat with electric mixer on medium speed 2 minutes, scraping bowl occasionally. Separate 1 egg. Add 3 eggs, 1 egg yolk and 1-1/2 cups flour to dough; reserve remaining egg white. Beat dough with electric mixer on high speed 2 minutes, scraping bowl occasionally. By hand, stir in enough of the remaining flour to make a soft dough. On a lightly floured board, knead dough 8 to 10 minutes or until smooth and elastic. Cover and let stand 20 minutes. Divide dough in half. Divide each half into 3 equal pieces. Roll each piece into a 24-inch rope. On 1 greased baking sheet, braid 3 ropes, then curve the braid to form a ring. Seal ends. Brush ring with oil. Cover. Repeat with remaining 3 ropes on the second greased baking sheet. Refrigerate 2 to 24 hours. To bake, preheat oven to 375°F (190°C). Uncover rings and let stand at room temperature 10 minutes. Slightly beat reserved egg white. Brush rings with beaten egg white. Bake 20 to 25 minutes or until ring sounds hollow when tapped with your finger. Makes 2 rings.

How To Make Chocolate Macaroon Muffins

1/Fill muffin cups about 1/3 full with batter, then top with 2 teaspoons of creamy coconut filling and another spoonful of batter.

2/After baking, dip the tops of the warm muffin in melted butter or margarine, then roll the tops in a shallow dish of granulated sugar until they are coated.

Bubble Bread Photo on page 78.

It's fun to pull your own bubble off this sensational sweet bread.

Basic Sweet Dough, page 80
2/3 cup granulated sugar
1 teaspoon ground cinnamon
5 tablespoons butter or margarine, melted
2 tablespoons butter or margarine

1/2 cup brown sugar, firmly packed
2 tablespoons light corn syrup
1/4 teaspoon lemon extract
1/4 teaspoon maple flavoring

Prepare Basic Sweet Dough. Grease a 9-inch tube pan; set aside. Shape dough into about thirty 1-inch balls. In a pie plate, mix granulated sugar and cinnamon. Dip balls into 5 tablespoons melted butter or margarine, then roll in cinnamon-sugar mixture. Arrange balls in layers in the greased tube pan. Cover and let rise in a warm place about 40 minutes or until doubled in bulk. Preheat oven to 375°F (190°C). In a small saucepan, melt 2 tablespoons butter or margarine. Stir in brown sugar, corn syrup, lemon extract and maple flavoring. Pour brown sugar mixture over risen dough. Bake 35 minutes. Bread is done when it is no longer doughy; to be sure you may have to pull off a bubble. Cool in pan 10 minutes. Invert onto a platter; remove pan. Serve bread warm. Makes 1 ring.

Chocolate Macaroon Muffins

Condensed milk is used instead of egg whites in this muffin version of macaroons.

2 cups all-purpose flour
1/2 cup sugar
3 tablespoons unsweetened cocoa powder
1 tablespoon baking powder
1 teaspoon salt
1 egg, slightly beaten

1 cup milk
1/3 cup vegetable oil
Macaroon Filling, see below
1/2 cup butter or margarine, melted
1/2 cup sugar

Macaroon Filling:
1 cup flaked coconut
1/4 cup sweetened condensed milk

1/4 teaspoon almond extract

Preheat oven to 400°F (205°C). Grease bottoms of 12 muffin pan cups; set aside. In a medium bowl, mix flour, 1/2 cup sugar, cocoa powder, baking powder and salt. In a small bowl, mix egg, milk and oil. Make a well with a spoon in center of the flour mixture. Pour egg mixture into the well. Stir until flour mixture is moistened; batter will still be lumpy. Prepare Macaroon Filling. Gently spoon about half the chocolate batter into the greased muffin pan cups. Spoon about 2 teaspoons Macaroon Filling onto center of each muffin. Spoon remaining chocolate batter on top of Macaroon Filling. Bake 20 to 22 minutes or until muffins pull away from sides of cups. Immediately remove from pans. Dip tops of warm muffins in melted butter or margarine, then in remaining 1/2 cup sugar. Serve warm. Makes 12 muffins.

Macaroon Filling:
In a small bowl, mix coconut, sweetened condensed milk and almond extract. Stir until moistened.

Blue-Ribbon Blueberry Muffins

If you don't have blueberries, check the variations against your pantry stock.

2 cups all-purpose flour	3/4 cup milk
1/2 cup sugar	1/3 cup vegetable oil
1 tablespoon baking powder	1 cup fresh or thawed frozen blueberries
1 teaspoon salt	1/2 cup butter or margarine, melted
1 egg, slightly beaten	1/2 cup sugar

Preheat oven to 400°F (205°C). Grease bottoms of 12 muffin pan cups; set aside. In a medium bowl, mix flour, 1/2 cup sugar, baking powder and salt. In a small bowl, mix egg, milk and oil. Make a well with a spoon in center of the flour mixture. Pour egg mixture and blueberries into the well. Stir until flour mixture is moistened; the batter will still be lumpy. Gently spoon batter into the greased muffin pan cups, filling each 2/3 full. Bake 20 to 22 minutes or until golden brown. Immediately remove from muffin pan cups. Dip tops of warm muffins in melted butter or margarine, then in 1/2 cup sugar. Serve warm. Makes 12 muffins.

Variations

Apple-Cinnamon Crunch Muffins: Omit blueberries. Stir 1 cup grated apple, 1/4 cup golden raisins and 1/2 teaspoon ground cinnamon into flour mixture with egg mixture. In a small bowl, combine 2 tablespoons brown sugar, 2 tablespoons all-purpose flour and 1/4 teaspoon ground cinnamon. Cut in 1 tablespoon butter or margarine until crumbly. After spooning batter into muffin pan cups, sprinkle with brown sugar mixture. Omit dipping muffins in melted butter or margarine and sugar.
Cranberry-Orange Muffins: Omit blueberries. In a small bowl, mix 1 cup chopped cranberries, 1/4 cup sugar and 1 teaspoon grated orange peel. Stir cranberry mixture into flour mixture with egg mixture.
Date-Nut Muffins: Omit blueberries. Stir 3/4 cup diced pitted dates and 1/2 cup chopped nuts into flour mixture with egg mixture.
Miniature Muffins: Spoon any of the above batters into greased bite-size muffin pan cups. Bake at 400°F (205°C) 6 to 8 minutes or until golden brown.

Herbal Popovers

You'll want to make these often to go with You-Name-It a la King, page 103.

3 eggs	3 tablespoons butter or margarine, melted
1 cup milk	1 teaspoon dried thyme, sage or basil, crushed
1 cup all-purpose flour	1/2 teaspoon celery salt

Preheat oven to 450°F (230°C). Grease eight 6-ounce custard cups; set aside. In blender container, mix eggs, milk, flour, butter or margarine, thyme and celery salt. Cover and process at low speed until smooth. Spoon about 1/3 cup batter into each greased custard cup. Bake 15 minutes. Reduce heat to 375°F (190°C) and bake 30 minutes longer or until browned. Serve immediately. Makes 8 popovers.

Spiced Peach Muffins

Yogurt is the magic ingredient—it gives a delicate flavor and texture.

2 cups all-purpose flour
1/2 cup granulated sugar
1 tablespoon baking powder
1 teaspoon salt
1/2 teaspoon baking soda
1/2 teaspoon ground cinnamon
1/2 teaspoon ground nutmeg

Dash ground mace
1 egg, slightly beaten
1 (8-oz.) carton peach yogurt
1/3 cup milk
1/3 cup vegetable oil
1/2 cup finely chopped dried peaches
Crunch Topping, see below

Crunch Topping:
2 tablespoons all-purpose flour
2 tablespoons brown sugar
2 tablespoons chopped walnuts

1/2 teaspoon ground cinnamon
2 tablespoons butter or margarine

Preheat oven to 400°F (205°C). Grease bottoms of 12 muffin pan cups; set aside. In a medium bowl, mix flour, sugar, baking powder, salt, baking soda, cinnamon, nutmeg and mace. In a small bowl, mix egg, peach yogurt, milk and oil. Make a well with a spoon in center of the flour mixture. Pour egg mixture and chopped peaches into the well. Stir until flour mixture is moistened; the batter will still be lumpy. Gently spoon batter into the greased muffin pan cups, filling each 2/3 full. Prepare Crunch Topping. Sprinkle each muffin with about 2 teaspoons Crunch Topping. Bake 20 to 22 minutes or until golden brown. Remove from muffin pan cups; serve warm. Makes 12 muffins.

Crunch Topping:
In a small bowl, mix flour, brown sugar, walnuts and cinnamon. Cut in butter or margarine until crumbly.

Caramel-Pecan Sticky Buns <small>Photo on page 79.</small>

Sure they're sticky—but that's half the fun!

Basic Sweet Dough, page 80
3 tablespoons butter or margarine, melted
1 cup chopped pecans
1/2 cup brown sugar, firmly packed

1-1/2 teaspoons ground cinnamon
3/4 cup brown sugar, firmly packed
4 tablespoons butter or margarine, melted
2 tablespoons light corn syrup

Prepare Basic Sweet Dough. Grease a 13" x 9" baking dish; set aside. On a lightly floured board, roll out dough to a 15" x 12" rectangle. Brush with 3 tablespoons melted butter or margarine. In a small bowl, mix pecans, 1/2 cup brown sugar and cinnamon. Sprinkle pecan mixture evenly over dough. Roll up dough tightly from the long side, jelly-roll fashion; seal edges. Cut roll into fifteen 1-inch slices. In a small bowl, mix 3/4 cup brown sugar, 4 tablespoons melted butter or margarine and corn syrup. Spread mixture over bottom of the greased baking dish. Place rolls cut-side up on brown sugar mixture in baking dish. Cover and let rise in a warm place about 30 minutes or until doubled in bulk. Preheat oven to 375°F (190°C). Bake 25 to 30 minutes or until done. Cool in pan 10 minutes. Invert on a platter; remove pan. Serve buns warm. Makes 15 buns.

Banana-Nut Loaf

For a fabulous dessert, serve this coffeecake with a fluffy cream cheese icing.

1 cup granulated sugar	2 cups all-purpose flour
1/2 cup shortening	1 tablespoon baking powder
2 eggs	1/2 teaspoon salt
1 cup mashed ripe banana	3/4 cup chopped walnuts
1 teaspoon lemon juice	Powdered sugar

Preheat oven to 350°F (175°C). Grease a 9" x 5" loaf pan; set aside. In a large bowl, cream granulated sugar and shortening with electric mixer on high speed until mixture is light and fluffy. Add eggs 1 at a time, beating well after each addition. Stir in banana and lemon juice. In a medium bowl, mix flour, baking powder and salt. Stir into banana mixture. Beat with electric mixer on medium speed 1 minute. Fold in walnuts. Pour batter into the greased pan. Bake 1 hour or until golden brown. Cool in pan 10 minutes. Remove from pan and place on rack. Sift powdered sugar over top of loaf. Makes 1 loaf.

Fanned Apricot Coffeecake

You can fill this cheese-flavored coffeecake with your own favorite jam, jelly or preserves.

2-1/3 cups all-purpose flour	1/4 cup shortening
2 tablespoons sugar	1/2 cup milk
1 tablespoon baking powder	1/2 cup apricot preserves
1/2 teaspoon salt	1/4 cup chopped walnuts
1 (3-oz.) pkg. cream cheese, softened	Powdered Sugar Glaze, see below
6 tablespoons butter or margarine, softened	

Powdered Sugar Glaze:

1 cup powdered sugar	1/4 teaspoon vanilla extract
2 tablespoons milk	

Preheat oven to 400°F (205°C). Grease a baking sheet; set aside. In a medium bowl, stir together flour, sugar, baking powder and salt. With a pastry blender or 2 knives, cut in cream cheese, butter or margarine and shortening until mixture resembles coarse peas. Stir in milk. On a lightly floured board, knead dough gently 20 times. Place dough on waxed paper. Roll out to a 12" x 8" rectangle. Turn rectangle onto the greased baking sheet. Spread apricot preserves lengthwise to cover 2/3 of the rectangle; sprinkle with walnuts. Fold the third of the rectangle without preserves over the center. Fold over again, making 3 layers of dough and 2 layers of filling. Seal edges. From folded edge cut dough into 1-inch slices to within 1 inch of opposite side; twist strips so that cut side is up. Bake 25 minutes or until golden brown. Remove coffeecake from baking sheet. Cool on rack 10 minutes. Prepare Powdered Sugar Glaze. Drizzle glaze on warm coffeecake. Makes 1 coffeecake.

Powdered Sugar Glaze:
In a small bowl, mix powdered sugar, milk and vanilla. Beat until smooth.

Overnight Apple Cakes

Ready-to-bake coffeecakes spend the night in the refrigerator.

1/2 cup milk
1/2 cup butter or margarine
1/4 cup water
2-3/4 cups all-purpose flour
1/4 cup granulated sugar
1/2 teaspoon salt
1 pkg. active dry yeast

1 egg
1/2 cup chopped walnuts
1 (20-oz.) can apple slices, drained
3/4 cup butter or margarine
3/4 cup brown sugar, firmly packed
1-1/2 teaspoons ground cinnamon

Grease two 8-inch, round pans; set aside. In a medium saucepan, mix milk, 1/2 cup butter or margarine and water. Heat only until warm (120°F, 50°C); the butter does not need to melt. In a large bowl, mix 1/2 cup flour, granulated sugar, salt and yeast. Add warmed milk mixture. Beat with electric mixer on medium speed 2 minutes, scraping bowl occasionally. Add egg and 1 cup flour. Beat with electric mixer on high speed 2 minutes, scraping bowl occasionally. By hand, stir in walnuts and enough remaining flour to make a stiff batter. Cover and let stand 20 minutes. Spread dough evenly in the greased pans. Arrange drained apple slices on top of dough. Cover; refrigerate 2 to 24 hours. When ready to bake, preheat oven to 350°F (175°C). Uncover cakes; let stand at room temperature 10 minutes. Bake cakes 35 minutes. While cakes are baking, melt 3/4 cup butter or margarine in a small saucepan. Stir in brown sugar and cinnamon. Pour brown sugar mixture over cakes. Bake 15 minutes longer. Makes 2 coffeecakes.

How To Make Fanned Apricot Coffeecake

1/Roll out dough to a 12″ x 8″ rectangle. Spread apricot preserves across 8 inches of the 12-inch side. Fold the remaining 4 inches of dough over half of the preserve-covered dough. Fold over again, making an 8″ x 4″ rectangle.

2/Starting from the edge of dough with the fold, cut dough crosswise in 1-inch strips, cutting to within 1 inch of the opposite side. Slightly twist each strip of dough sideways to form a fan-shaped loaf.

Quick Blueberry Spirals

A fast fix-up for refrigerated biscuits. Use the extra pie filling as an ice cream topping.

2 (7.5-oz.) pkgs. refrigerated biscuits
   (10 biscuits each)
2 tablespoons butter or margarine, melted

1/4 cup sugar
2/3 cup canned blueberry pie filling
Powdered Sugar Glaze, see below

Powdered Sugar Glaze:
1/2 cup powdered sugar
1 tablespoon milk

1/8 teaspoon vanilla extract

Preheat oven to 400°F (205°C). Grease a baking sheet; set aside. On a lightly floured board, separate biscuits into 10 stacks of 2 biscuits each. With your hands, roll each stack into a 14-inch rope. Brush with melted butter or margarine and roll in sugar. On the greased baking sheet, gently coil 1 roll into a spiral. Repeat with remaining rolls. Flatten each spiral with a spatula. Bake 12 minutes or until golden brown. Remove and cool on rack 10 minutes. Top each spiral with about 1 tablespoon blueberry pie filling. Prepare Powdered Sugar Glaze. Drizzle warm rolls with glaze. Makes 10 spirals.

Powdered Sugar Glaze:
In a small bowl, mix powdered sugar, milk and vanilla. Beat until smooth.

Cinnamon Twist Coffeecake *Photo on page 78.*

Brunch guests always marvel at this unusually shaped coffeecake.

Basic Sweet Dough, page 80
3 tablespoons butter or margarine, melted
1/2 cup brown sugar, firmly packed

1-1/2 teaspoons ground cinnamon
1/2 cup seedless raisins
Powdered Sugar Glaze, see below

Powdered Sugar Glaze:
1 cup powdered sugar
2 tablespoons milk

1/4 teaspoon vanilla extract

Prepare Basic Sweet Dough. Grease a 9-inch square pan; set aside. On a lightly floured board, roll out dough to a 12-inch square. Brush lightly with melted butter or margarine. In a small bowl, mix brown sugar and cinnamon. Sprinkle a strip down center third of square with half the cinnamon-sugar mixture, then sprinkle with half the raisins. Fold one third of dough over center third. Sprinkle the double layer of dough with remaining cinnamon-sugar mixture and raisins. Fold remaining third of dough over; seal edge. Cut crosswise into twelve 1-inch strips. Holding the ends of each strip, twist tightly in opposite directions. Arrange 2 rows of 6 twists each in the greased pan. Cover; let rise in a warm place about 30 minutes or until doubled in bulk. Preheat oven to 375°F (190°C). Bake coffeecake 25 to 30 minutes or until golden brown. Cool in pan 10 minutes. While cooling, prepare Powdered Sugar Glaze. Place coffeecake on a platter. Drizzle Powdered Sugar Glaze on warm coffeecake. Makes 1 coffeecake.

Powdered Sugar Glaze:
In a small bowl, mix powdered sugar, milk and vanilla. Beat until smooth.

Meats

How much meat to buy is a question that puzzles many cooks. The answer depends on the appetites of your guests and the amount of bone in the cut you are buying. Here are some general guidelines:

Type of Meat	Amount Per Serving
Boneless meat	1/4 to 1/3 pound
Boneless roasts	1/3 to 1/2 pound
Small bone-in such as ham	1/2 pound
Large bone-in such as spareribs	3/4 to 1 pound

Use fresh meats within 2 to 3 days. Ground meat and variety meats should be used within 24 hours. Store cured, smoked and ready-to-serve meats in the original wrappings. Store fresh prepackaged meat in the original wrapping if you plan to use it within 1 or 2 days. To keep prepackaged meat longer, loosen the ends of the wrapping or wrap it loosely in waxed paper, clear plastic wrap or aluminum foil. Meats, of course, should not be washed.

If you think of ham as the perfect brunch meat, Ham With Peach Glaze, page 20, was created with you in mind.

If it takes steak to make a party at your house, try Tangy Marinated Steaks on page 16. Steak doesn't always mean last-minute cooking. The day before the brunch, put together the Marinated Steak Salad, see page 98, and enjoy steak in a spectacular new way.

Smoked Pork Chops O'Brien

Meat and potatoes baked together in a cheese sauce.

3 cups frozen hash brown O'Brien-style
   potatoes, thawed
1 (3-oz.) can sliced mushrooms, drained
1/2 teaspoon dried thyme, crushed
1/2 teaspoon dried basil, crushed
1 (11-oz.) can condensed Cheddar cheese soup

1/4 cup milk
1 teaspoon Worcestershire sauce
Steak sauce
6 smoked pork chops (2 lbs.)
6 green pepper rings

Preheat oven to 375°F (190°C). In a large bowl, mix potatoes, mushrooms, thyme and basil. Fold in soup, milk and Worcestershire sauce. Turn mixture into an 11" x 7" baking dish. Spread steak sauce on pork chops. Overlap pork chops on the potato mixture. Top each chop with a green pepper ring. Cover and bake 1 hour or until heated through. Let stand 10 minutes. Makes 6 servings.

Smokehouse Quartet

Have the meats ready and in the chafing dish so all that's left to do is make the glaze.

3 tablespoons butter or margarine
2 apples, cored, sliced
1 teaspoon ground cinnamon
1/4 teaspoon ground nutmeg
1 tablespoon cornstarch

1 cup cranberry-apple juice
6 small, thick ham slices
6 sausage patties, cooked, drained
12 link sausages, cooked, drained
12 oz. smoked sausage, cut in chunks

In a small skillet, melt butter or margarine. Add apple slices and sprinkle with cinnamon and nutmeg. Cook over medium heat until apple slices are tender, stirring occasionally. Remove apple slices and set aside, reserving juices in skillet. Blend cornstarch into juices. Add cranberry-apple juice. Stir constantly over medium-high heat until mixture thickens and bubbles. In a chafing dish or large skillet, arrange meats and apple slices. Pour cranberry glaze over meats and apple slices. Cover and heat through. Makes 8 servings.

Bacon & Egg Salad Stack-Ups

Leftovers? Arrange them between thick slices of bread for a divine Dagwood sandwich.

3 Hard-Cooked Eggs, page 74, chopped
2 tablespoons mayonnaise or salad dressing
1 tablespoon sweet pickle relish
2 teaspoons prepared mustard
1/2 teaspoon prepared horseradish

12 slices Canadian bacon,
  cut 1/4-inch thick (1 lb.)
6 thick tomato slices
2 (10-oz.) pkgs. frozen broccoli
  in cheese sauce

Preheat oven to 350°F (175°C). In a medium bowl, mix eggs, mayonnaise or salad dressing, relish, mustard and horseradish. Place 6 bacon slices in an 11" x 7" baking dish. On each slice, layer a spoonful of egg salad, another slice of bacon and a slice of tomato. Cover and bake 25 to 30 minutes or until heated through. While stack-ups are baking, prepare broccoli according to package directions. Drain pan juices from stack-ups. Spoon broccoli over stack-ups. Makes 6 servings.

Fluffy Mustard Sauce

If you take this on a picnic, keep it in the cooler until serving time.

2 egg yolks
1/2 teaspoon salt
Dash pepper
1-1/2 teaspoons white wine tarragon vinegar

1 cup vegetable oil
1-1/2 teaspoons lemon juice
2 tablespoons Dijon-style mustard
1 tablespoon honey

In a small bowl, beat together egg yolks, salt and pepper with electric mixer on medium speed until blended. Beat in vinegar. Add oil 1 teaspoon at a time until 1/4 cup has been added, beating with electric mixer on high speed after each addition. Alternately add remaining oil 1/4 cup at a time and lemon juice, beating at high speed after each addition. Beat in mustard and honey. Refrigerate until serving time. Makes 1-1/4 cups of sauce.

Orange-Glazed Canadian Bacon

You can make thick supper sandwiches with leftover Canadian bacon.

1 (3-lb.) piece Canadian bacon
1/2 cup brown sugar, firmly packed
1 tablespoon all-purpose flour
1 teaspoon dry mustard
1/2 teaspoon grated orange peel

1/4 teaspoon ground cinnamon
1/4 teaspoon ground allspice
2 tablespoons orange juice
1 orange, thinly sliced

Preheat oven to 350°F (175°C). Place Canadian bacon in an 11" x 7" baking dish. Bake 1 hour 20 minutes. In a small bowl, mix brown sugar, flour, dry mustard, orange peel, cinnamon and allspice. Stir in orange juice. Spoon half the orange glaze over Canadian bacon and top with orange slices. Bake 10 to 30 minutes longer or until meat thermometer reaches 160°F (70°C), basting with remaining glaze several times. Cut in thick slices. Makes 8 to 10 servings.

Herb-Buttered Breakfast Steaks

Superb for breakfast with eggs or on French bread as an open-faced sandwich.

4 tablespoons butter or margarine
1 small onion, sliced, separated into rings
1 medium green pepper, cut in strips
1/2 teaspoon dried basil, crushed
1/2 teaspoon dried oregano, crushed

1/2 teaspoon dried thyme, crushed
1 lb. beef cubed steaks or minute steaks,
 1/4 inch thick (4 steaks)
Garlic salt

In a large skillet, melt butter or margarine. Add onion, green pepper, basil, oregano and thyme. Stir frequently over medium-high heat until tender. Remove vegetables from skillet; keep warm on a platter. Add steaks to skillet. Sprinkle with garlic salt. Cook, turning once, until done as desired, about 4 minutes for rare. Place steaks on platter. Drizzle with pan juices. Makes 4 servings.

Ham Ring Español

Grind leftover ham to make this spicy ring.

4 eggs, slightly beaten
2 cups soft breadcrumbs, page 77
1/2 cup chopped onion
1/2 cup chopped green pepper
1/2 cup chili sauce
2 teaspoons dry mustard

1-1/4 lbs. ground cooked ham
1-1/4 lbs. ground pork
1/2 cup chili sauce
2 tablespoons brown sugar
1 teaspoon dry mustard

Preheat oven to 350°F (175°C). Oil a 6-1/2-cup ring mold; set aside. In a large bowl, mix eggs, breadcrumbs, onion, green pepper, 1/2 cup chili sauce and 2 teaspoons dry mustard. Add ground ham and ground pork; mix thoroughly. Pat mixture into the oiled mold. Invert onto a shallow baking pan. Remove mold. Bake 1-1/4 hours. While ring is baking, mix remaining ingredients in a small bowl. Spoon sauce over ring and bake 15 minutes longer. Makes 8 servings.

Continental Mixed Grill

Use fresh or canned peaches and your favorite chutney for this quick and unusual dish.

8 oz. chicken livers	8 slices thick-sliced bacon
12 oz. bulk pork sausage	Garlic salt
4 loin lamb chops, cut 1-1/2 inches thick	4 cling peach halves
(1-1/4 lbs.)	Chutney

Preheat broiler at moderate temperature. Place chicken livers in the bottom of a large broiler pan; place broiler rack over chicken livers. Shape sausage into four 1-inch thick patties. Place patties, lamb chops and bacon on broiler rack. Broil 3 to 5 inches from heat 7 minutes. Turn chops and patties over. Remove bacon; drain on paper towels and keep warm. Broil chops and patties 3 minutes longer. Sprinkle with garlic salt. Place peach halves on broiler rack. Spoon chutney into center of peach halves. Broil 2 to 3 minutes or until peaches are heated through and meats are done. If you prefer chicken livers well done, place them on the broiler rack and cook a few minutes longer. Makes 4 to 6 servings.

Dilled Ham Roll-Ups

Pour a rich cheese sauce over deviled eggs wrapped in slices of ham.

8 Hard-Cooked Eggs, page 74	1 (10-oz.) pkg. frozen green peas
3 tablespoons mayonnaise or salad dressing	with cream sauce
2 tablespoons bacon bits	Water
1 teaspoon prepared mustard	Butter or margarine
1 teaspoon cider vinegar	1 envelope cheese sauce mix
1/8 teaspoon salt	1 cup milk
1/8 teaspoon prepared horseradish	1 (3-oz.) can sliced mushrooms, drained
Dash pepper	1 (2-oz.) jar chopped pimiento, drained
8 thin ham slices	1 teaspoon dried dillweed

Preheat oven to 375°F (190°C). Cut Hard-Cooked Eggs in half lengthwise; remove yolks and place in a small bowl. Add mayonnaise or salad dressing, bacon bits, mustard, vinegar, salt, horseradish and pepper. Using a fork to mash yolks, mix thoroughly. Fill egg whites with yolk mixture. Place 2 egg halves end-to-end on each ham slice; roll up. Place roll-ups in a 10" x 6" baking dish. In a medium saucepan, cook peas with water and butter or margarine according to package directions. Stir constantly over high heat until boiling. Remove from heat. Add cheese sauce mix. Stir until smooth. Add milk. Return to heat. Stir constantly over medium-high heat until mixture thickens and bubbles. Stir in mushrooms, pimiento and dillweed. Spoon creamed peas over roll-ups. Bake 30 minutes. Makes 4 servings.

> *Using a meat thermometer will banish a lot of guesswork. Roast rare beef and cooked or canned ham to 140°F (60°C), medium beef to 160°F (70°C), and well-done beef and fresh pork to 170°F (75°C).*

Smoky Beef & Broccoli Stack-Ups

Herbed pastry rounds and broccoli spears under a smoked beef and cheese sauce. Delicious!

2 sticks pie crust mix
1/2 teaspoon dried thyme, crushed
1/2 teaspoon dried marjoram, crushed
1/2 teaspoon celery seeds
Water
1/4 cup butter or margarine
1 cup chopped zucchini
1/3 cup chopped onion
1/3 cup all-purpose flour

1 cup milk
1 cup chicken broth
1 (4-oz.) carton semisoft natural cheese
   with pepper
1 (3-oz.) pkg. smoked sliced beef, snipped
1/4 cup chopped pimiento
2 (10-oz.) pkgs. frozen broccoli spears,
   cooked, drained

Preheat oven to 450°F (230°C). Place pie crust sticks in a medium bowl with thyme, marjoram and celery seeds. Add water according to package directions. Roll out half the dough on a lightly floured board. Cut into three 5-1/2-inch rounds. Repeat with remaining half of dough. Prick pastry rounds. Place on a baking sheet. Bake 8 to 10 minutes or until lightly browned. In a medium saucepan, melt butter or margarine; add zucchini and onion. Cook until barely tender. Blend in flour; add milk and chicken broth. Stir constantly over medium-high heat until mixture thickens and bubbles. Stir in cheese until melted. Stir in smoked beef and pimiento; heat through. To serve, place a baked pastry round on each of 6 plates. Place well-drained broccoli spears on pastry rounds. Spoon hot beef mixture over broccoli. Makes 6 servings.

Hobnob Hash Pie

Corned beef and cabbage in a hash-brown pie shell. Unusual and unusually good!

1/4 cup butter or margarine
1 (12-oz.) pkg. frozen shredded hash browns,
   thawed
Salt and pepper to taste
3 cups finely shredded cabbage
1/2 cup chopped onion
1/2 cup shredded carrot
1/2 cup chopped green pepper

3 tablespoons butter or margarine
2 eggs, beaten
1 (10-oz.) can cream of onion soup
1/3 cup all-purpose flour
1 tablespoon Dijon-style mustard
1 tablespoon prepared horseradish
1 (12-oz.) can corned beef, chopped

Preheat oven to 350°F (175°C). In a large oven-proof skillet, melt 1/4 cup butter or margarine. Pack hash browns into skillet and cook over low heat until bottom is browned. Sprinkle with salt and pepper. In another skillet, combine cabbage, onion, carrot, green pepper and remaining 3 tablespoons butter or margarine. Cook until vegetables are just tender drain if necessary. In a large bowl, combine eggs, soup, flour, mustard and horseradish. Stir in cabbage mixture. Top hash browns with corned beef, then cabbage mixture. Bake 40 to 45 minutes or until set. Let stand 10 minutes before serving. Cut in wedges to serve. Makes 6 to 8 servings.

Jazzy Hash Ring

You'll be amazed at what you can do with a can of corned beef hash and a few staples.

2 tablespoons butter or margarine
1/2 cup chopped onion
1/4 cup chopped green pepper
1/4 cup ketchup
1 tablespoon Worcestershire sauce
2 teaspoons prepared mustard

2 teaspoons prepared horseradish
2 (15-oz.) cans corned beef hash
6 eggs
1/2 cup shredded process American cheese
  (2 oz.)
Snipped parsley

Preheat oven to 350°F (175°C). Grease a 6-1/2 cup ring mold; set aside. In a large saucepan, melt butter or margarine. Add onion and green pepper. Cook over medium-high heat until tender, stirring occasionally. Stir in ketchup, Worcestershire sauce, mustard and horseradish; mix well. Stir in corned beef hash; mix well. Press hash mixture into greased mold. With a spoon, make 6 depressions in top of hash ring. Break an egg into each depression. Bake 35 to 45 minutes or until eggs are just set. Sprinkle with cheese and snipped parsley. Bake 1 to 2 minutes longer or until cheese melts. Makes 6 servings.

How To Make Jazzy Hash Ring

1/Mix corned beef hash with the mustard and horseradish mixture. Press into a greased 6-1/2-cup ring mold.

2/Make depressions in the hash ring with the back of a spoon. Then carefully slip an egg from a custard cup into each depression. Bake until the eggs are set.

Relish-Stuffed Flank Steaks

After rolling up the steak, press any stray stuffing back into the roll.

2/3 cup white wine vinegar
1/2 cup water
1/4 cup sugar
2 teaspoons celery salt
1 cup chopped onion
1 tomato, diced

1/2 cucumber, peeled, seeded, chopped
1/4 cup chopped green pepper
1-1/4 to 1-1/2 lb. beef flank steak
Instant non-seasoned meat tenderizer
1/4 cup sweet pickle relish

In a medium bowl, mix vinegar, water, sugar and celery salt. Stir in onion, tomato, cucumber and green pepper. Place steak on a board. With a meat mallet, pound steak evenly until about 1/2 inch thick. Score steak diagonally with a sharp knife, making a pattern of diamond shapes. Place steak in a plastic bag in an 11" x 7" baking dish. Pour vegetable mixture over steak. Close bag. Marinate in the refrigerator 8 hours or overnight. Preheat broiler at moderate temperature. Remove meat from marinade. Use meat tenderizer according to package directions. Drain vegetables. Stir relish into vegetables. Spread vegetable mixture evenly over steak. Roll up like a jelly-roll starting at the narrow end. Skewer roll with wooden picks at 1-inch intervals. Cut in 1-inch slices. Broil 3 to 5 inches from heat 8 minutes. Turn and broil 7 minutes or until done as desired. Makes 6 servings.

Marinated Steak Salad

Here's how to use leftover steak—and it's so good you'll plan it that way!

2 lbs. beef sirloin steak
3 cups sliced fresh mushrooms
1 (14-oz.) can artichoke hearts,
    drained, halved
1-1/3 cups vegetable oil
1 cup white wine vinegar
2 tablespoons finely chopped green onion
1 tablespoon Dijon-style mustard

1 tablespoon prepared horseradish
1/2 teaspoon celery salt
Dash garlic powder
Shredded lettuce
Avocado slices
Cherry tomatoes
Snipped parsley

Broil or grill steak until done as desired. Cut in 1/4-inch slices. In an 11" x 7" baking dish, place steak slices, mushrooms and artichokes. In a screw-top jar, mix oil, vinegar, green onion, mustard, horseradish, celery salt and garlic powder; shake well. Pour over steak and vegetables. Cover and refrigerate 8 hours or overnight, stirring occasionally. Before serving, arrange shredded lettuce on a platter. Drain steak, reserving marinade. Arrange steak, mushrooms, artichoke halves, avocado slices and cherry tomatoes on lettuce. Drizzle with reserved marinade. Sprinkle with parsley. Makes 4 servings.

For even heating, broil meats at moderate temperature settings. If your broiler is not calibrated, move the broiler rack to a lower level, 3 to 4 inches from the heating element.

Poultry

Chicken and turkey are so versatile, they lend themselves beautifully to savory sauces, stuffings and marinades. For elegance, choose Champagne-Glazed Chicken or Crab-Stuffed Chicken with Shrimp Newburg Sauce.

If you are lucky enough to own a clay baking pot, get it out for Turkey Breast Supreme. Cooking in a clay pot is different and easy, and you'll get delicious results. Be sure to follow the manufacturer's instructions for using the pot.

Many poultry dishes benefit from a waiting time to blend the flavors. Some of these recipes can be prepared completely the day before—for example, delightful Deviled Chicken Strata, Chicken & Wild Rice Croquettes and flavorful Chicken Tettrazini. In many other recipes you can make the sauce ahead and refrigerate it until it's time to reheat it or complete the preparation.

To store fresh poultry, remove the giblets, wrap them loosely and refrigerate them. Cook them as soon as possible. Wrap the poultry loosely in freezer wrap, heavy-duty foil or heavy-weight plastic freezer bags and keep it in the coldest part of your refrigerator. Use refrigerated poultry within 1 to 2 days.

One 4- to 5-pound stewing chicken yields about 5 cups of diced cooked chicken. When you stew a 3- to 4-pound broiler-fryer, count on 3 to 4 cups of diced cooked chicken. One (5-ounce) can of boned chicken equals about 1/2 cup of diced chicken. One (3-1/4-ounce) can whole chicken yields about 2-1/2 cups of diced chicken.

Champagne-Glazed Chicken

A spirited main dish for an extra-special Sunday brunch.

4 tablespoons butter or margarine
6 chicken breasts, boned
Salt and pepper to taste
1-1/2 cups champagne

1/4 cup peach brandy
1 (16-oz.) can sliced peaches
1 (8-oz.) can grapes
3 tablespoons cornstarch

Preheat oven to 375°F (190°C). In a 13" x 9" baking dish, melt butter or margarine. Place chicken in baking dish, turning to coat with melted butter or margarine. Season to taste with salt and pepper. Bake 30 to 40 minutes or until browned. Drain off pan juices. Pour champagne and brandy into baking dish. Drain peaches and grapes, reserving 1 cup peach syrup. Add peaches and grapes to chicken in baking dish. Bake 15 minutes or until chicken is tender. Remove chicken and fruits from baking dish and arrange on a platter; keep warm. Reserve pan juices. In a medium saucepan, mix cornstarch and 1/4 cup reserved peach syrup. Add remaining 3/4 cup peach syrup and 1-1/2 cups pan juices. Stir constantly over medium-high heat until mixture thickens and bubbles. Serve champagne sauce over chicken. Makes 6 servings.

Plantation Shortcake

If you love cornbread, have a brunch this weekend so you can enjoy this right away.

1 (10-oz.) pkg. cornbread mix
1 (8-3/4-oz.) can cream-style corn
1/2 cup shredded natural Swiss cheese
   (2 oz.)
2 eggs, slightly beaten
2 tablespoons milk

2 teaspoons prepared mustard
1 (14-oz.) can artichoke hearts,
   drained, chopped
1 (3-oz.) can chopped mushrooms, drained
1 cup shredded natural Swiss cheese (4 oz.)
Plantation Cream Sauce, see below

Plantation Cream Sauce:
2 tablespoons butter or margarine
2 tablespoons all-purpose flour
3/4 cup chicken broth
3/4 cup half-and-half

2 egg yolks, slightly beaten
1 cup cubed cooked chicken or turkey
1 cup cubed cooked ham

Preheat oven to 350°F (175°C). Grease an 8-inch square baking dish. In a medium bowl, mix cornbread mix, corn, 1/2 cup cheese, eggs, milk and mustard. Spread about 1 cup batter in the greased baking dish. In a medium bowl, mix artichokes, mushrooms and remaining 1 cup cheese. Spoon over batter in baking dish. Top with remaining batter. Bake 35 minutes or until cornbread is golden brown and has pulled away from sides of dish. Let stand 10 minutes before cutting into squares. Prepare Plantation Cream Sauce. Ladle sauce over cornbread squares. Makes 6 to 8 servings.

Plantation Cream Sauce:
In a medium saucepan, melt butter or margarine. Blend in flour. Add chicken broth and half-and-half. Stir constantly over medium-high heat until sauce thickens and bubbles. Blend 3/4 cup sauce into beaten egg yolks; mix well. Add egg yolk mixture to hot sauce. Stir in chicken and ham. Stir constantly over medium-high heat until heated through. Keep warm. Makes 2 cups of sauce.

Turkey Breast Supreme

The clay baking pot guarantees juiciness. Put one on your "want" list.

1/2 cup chopped celery
1/2 cup chopped carrot
1/2 cup chopped onion
1 (4-lb.) frozen turkey breast, thawed

4 tablespoons butter or margarine, melted
1 teaspoon dried sage
1 teaspoon dried thyme
1 teaspoon dried marjoram

Soak a clay baking pot and its lid in cold water 20 minutes. Remove pot and lid from water. Mix celery, carrot and onion in bottom of the pot. Place turkey breast on top of vegetables. Insert a meat thermometer in the thickest portion of the turkey breast so that it is not touching bone. In a small bowl, mix remaining ingredients; spoon over turkey. Cover pot with lid and place in *cold oven.* Set oven temperature at 450°F (230°C). Roast 1-1/2 hours or until interior temperature of turkey reaches 175°F (80°C). Serve pan juices separately. Makes 8 to 10 servings.

Deviled Chicken Strata

Make this the day before and refrigerate it until an hour before brunch is served.

4 cups herb-seasoned croutons
3 cups cubed cooked chicken
1/2 cup chopped celery
1/2 cup chopped green pepper
1/2 cup chopped onion
1/4 cup chopped pimiento

3/4 cup mayonnaise or salad dressing
2 teaspoons prepared mustard
1 cup shredded Swiss cheese (4 oz.)
4 eggs, slightly beaten
2 cups half-and-half

Place 2 cups croutons in an 11" x 7" baking dish; set aside. In a large bowl, mix chicken, celery, green pepper, onion and pimiento. Fold in mayonnaise or salad dressing and mustard. Spread chicken mixture over croutons in the baking dish. Top with cheese and remaining croutons. In a medium bowl, combine eggs and half-and-half. Beat with a fork or whisk until mixed well but not frothy. Pour egg mixture over croutons in the baking dish. Cover and refrigerate 2 to 24 hours. Preheat oven to 375°F (190°C). Bake casserole, uncovered 60 minutes or until set. Let stand 10 minutes before serving. Makes 8 servings.

Chicken & Wild Rice Croquettes

If you have trouble shaping cones, try cylinders, balls or patties.

1/2 cup wild rice
1 cup water
1 tablespoon butter or margarine
1 teaspoon dried thyme
1 teaspoon dried marjoram
1/2 teaspoon salt
4 slices bacon
3 tablespoons chopped onion
2 tablespoons all-purpose flour
1/4 teaspoon celery salt
3/4 cup half-and-half

3 egg yolks, slightly beaten
1 tablespoon snipped parsley
1/2 teaspoon salt
1 cup finely chopped cooked
    chicken or shrimp
Vegetable oil for deep frying
1/4 cup all-purpose flour
1 egg, beaten
1/2 cup fine dry seasoned breadcrumbs,
    page 77

Rinse wild rice. In a medium saucepan, combine water, rice, butter or margarine, thyme, marjoram and 1/2 teaspoon salt. Bring to a boil. Reduce heat, cover and simmer 50 to 60 minutes or until rice is tender. While rice is cooking, fry bacon in a medium skillet over medium-high heat until crisp. Drain bacon on paper towels. Reserve 3 tablespoons drippings in skillet. Crumble bacon and set aside. Cook onion in reserved drippings until tender. Blend in 2 tablespoons flour and celery salt. In a medium bowl, mix half-and-half, 3 egg yolks, parsley and remaining 1/2 teaspoon salt. Stir into flour mixture in skillet. Stir constantly over medium-high heat until thickened and bubbly. Fold in rice, chicken or shrimp and crumbled bacon. Cover and refrigerate at least 4 hours. With your hands, shape 1/4 cup mixture into a solid cone. Repeat with remaining mixture. Heat oil for deep frying to 365°F (185°C); at this temperature a 1-inch cube of bread dropped into oil will turn golden brown in 50 to 60 seconds. Roll croquettes first in 1/4 cup flour, then in beaten egg and then in breadcrumbs. Fry 3 or 4 at a time in hot oil 2 to 3 minutes or until browned. Drain on paper towels. Serve immediately or keep warm in oven. Makes 9 croquettes or 4 to 5 servings.

You-Name-It a la King

So versatile you can substitute cooked fish, tuna fish or hard-cooked eggs for the poultry.

6 tablespoons butter or margarine
1/4 cup shredded carrot
1/4 cup chopped celery
1/4 cup chopped onion
1/3 cup all-purpose flour
1/2 teaspoon salt
1 cup chicken broth

1 cup half-and-half
2 cups cubed cooked chicken or turkey
1 (3-oz.) can sliced mushrooms, drained
1 (2-oz.) jar pimiento, chopped
Herbal Popovers, page 86, toast triangles or
    baked patty shells

In a medium saucepan, melt butter or margarine. Add carrot, celery and onion. Cook over medium-high heat until vegetables are tender, stirring occasionally. Blend in flour and salt. Add broth and half-and-half. Stir constantly over medium-high heat until mixture thickens and bubbles. Stir in chicken or turkey, mushrooms and pimiento. Cover and cook until mixture is heated through. Serve in Herbal Popovers, over toast triangles or in patty shells. Makes 4 servings.

Oriental Chicken Salad

Look for five-spice powder in gourmet or oriental food shops—or you can make your own.

1/4 cup sesame oil
1/4 cup soy sauce
1 teaspoon Five-Spice Powder, see below
1 teaspoon prepared mustard
1/4 teaspoon hot pepper sauce
2 large chicken breasts, cooked, skinned,
    boned (about 2-1/3 cups)

1 (6-oz.) pkg. frozen pea pods,
    cooked, drained
1/4 cup chopped green onion
1 (3-oz.) can rice noodles
1/4 cup chopped toasted almonds
Shredded romaine
Preserved kumquats

Five-Spice Powder:
1 teaspoon ground cinnamon
1 teaspoon crushed aniseed
1/4 teaspoon crushed fennel

1/4 teaspoon freshly ground pepper
1/8 teaspoon ground cloves

In a large bowl, mix sesame oil, soy sauce, Five-Spice Powder, mustard and hot pepper sauce; set aside. Cut chicken into thin strips. Add chicken, pea pods and green onion to soy mixture; toss. Refrigerate until serving time. Before serving, toss rice noodles and almonds with chicken mixture. Arrange shredded romaine on individual plates. Top with chicken mixture. Garnish with preserved kumquats. Makes 4 servings.

Five-Spice Powder:
Combine all ingredients in a small bowl. Mix well. Store in an airtight container in a dark cupboard.

Chicken Tettrazini

Spaghetti and poultry baked in a rich mushroom sauce.

10 slices bacon
1 cup sliced fresh mushrooms
1/2 cup chopped onion
1/2 cup all-purpose flour
1 teaspoon salt
1/4 teaspoon pepper
1 (13-3/4-oz.) can chicken broth

2 cups half-and-half
3 to 4 tablespoons dry sherry
9 oz. spaghetti, cooked, drained
3 cups cubed cooked chicken
3/4 cup grated Parmesan cheese
Paprika
Snipped parsley

Preheat oven to 375°F (190°C). In a large skillet, cook bacon over medium-high heat until crisp. Drain on paper towels. Reserve 1/2 cup drippings in the skillet. Crumble bacon and set aside. Cook mushrooms and onion in drippings over medium-high heat until tender, stirring occasionally. Blend in flour, salt and pepper. Add chicken broth and half-and-half. Stir constantly over medium-high heat until mixture thickens and bubbles. Remove from heat. Stir in sherry. In a 13" x 9" baking dish, mix spaghetti, chicken, crumbled bacon and 1/2 cup Parmesan cheese. Pour cream sauce over spaghetti mixture. Sprinkle with remaining Parmesan cheese and paprika. Bake 30 minutes or until heated through. Garnish with snipped parsley. Makes 8 servings.

Bombay Curried Chicken

Condiments for curry: chopped peanuts, shredded coconut, raisins and chopped hard-cooked eggs.

4 tablespoons butter or margarine
1 cup chopped, peeled apple
1/3 cup chopped celery
1/4 cup chopped onion
2 teaspoons curry powder
1 cup sliced banana
3 tablespoons all-purpose flour
1/2 teaspoon salt

1 (13-3/4-oz.) can chicken broth
1/4 cup dry white wine
1/4 cup half-and-half
2 cups cubed cooked chicken
1 (8-oz.) can sliced pineapple,
    drained, quartered
Hot cooked rice

In a medium saucepan, melt butter or margarine. Add apple, celery, onion and curry powder. Cook over medium-high heat until vegetables are tender, stirring occasionally. Stir in sliced banana, flour and salt. Add chicken broth. Stir constantly over medium-high heat until mixture thickens and bubbles. Stir in first the wine, then the half-and-half. Add chicken and pineapple. Cover and cook until mixture is heated through. Serve over rice with curry condiments, if desired. Makes 4 to 6 servings.

Chicken Salad Véronique

Be sure to allow enough time for the coated grapes to dry.

3 cups cubed cooked chicken
1 cup seedless green grapes, halved
1/2 cup toasted slivered almonds
1/2 cup chopped celery
3 tablespoons chopped onion
1/2 teaspoon celery salt

1/3 cup mayonnaise or salad dressing
1/3 cup lemon yogurt
1 tablespoon dry white wine
1/2 teaspoon prepared mustard
Frosted Grape Clusters, see below
Leaf lettuce

Frosted Grape Clusters:
6 seedless green grape clusters
1 egg white, beaten

1 (3-oz.) pkg. lime-flavored gelatin

In a medium bowl, mix chicken, halved grapes, almonds, celery, onion and celery salt. In a small bowl, mix mayonnaise or salad dressing, yogurt, wine and mustard. Fold mayonnaise mixture into chicken mixture. Refrigerate until serving time. Before serving, prepare Frosted Grape Clusters. Arrange lettuce leaves on individual plates. Spoon chicken salad onto lettuce leaves. Garnish with Frosted Grape Clusters. Makes 6 servings.

Frosted Grape Clusters:
Brush grape clusters with egg white or dip into egg white. Sprinkle with lime-flavored gelatin. Dry on a wire rack.

How To Make Chicken Salad Véronique

1/To make Frosted Grape Clusters, brush small bunches of green or red grapes with beaten egg white.

2/Sprinkle the coated grapes with your favorite flavored dry gelatin or granulated sugar. Dry completely on a rack.

Crab-Stuffed Chicken

Pour Shrimp Newburg Sauce over tender chicken stuffed with mushrooms and crabmeat.

2 tablespoons butter or margarine
1/4 cup finely chopped green onion
1 cup cooked crabmeat
1 (3-oz.) can chopped mushrooms, drained
1/2 cup coarsely crushed saltine
    cracker crumbs
2 tablespoons snipped parsley
2 tablespoons dry white wine

1/2 teaspoon salt
4 (5-oz.) whole chicken breasts,
    boned, skinned
Vegetable oil
Shrimp Newburg Sauce, see below
Hot cooked rice
Snipped parsley
Paprika

Shrimp Newburg Sauce:
2 tablespoons butter or margarine
2 tablespoons all-purpose flour
1/4 teaspoon salt
1/4 teaspoon paprika

1-1/2 cups half-and-half
1 cup shelled cooked shrimp
2 tablespoons dry sherry

Preheat oven to 375°F (190°C). In a medium skillet, melt butter or margarine. Add green onion. Cook over medium-high heat until tender, stirring occasionally. Stir in crabmeat, mushrooms, cracker crumbs, 2 tablespoons snipped parsley, wine and salt; mix well. Spoon about 1/3 cup stuffing mixture onto each chicken breast. Fold 2 sides in, roll up and tie with string. Place in a baking pan. Brush chicken with oil. Cover and bake 30 minutes or until tender. While chicken is cooking, prepare Shrimp Newburg Sauce. To serve, remove string from cooked chicken breasts. Place chicken breasts on top of hot rice on individual plates. Spoon about 1/2 cup Shrimp Newburg Sauce over each chicken breast. Sprinkle with parsley and paprika. Makes 4 servings.

Shrimp Newburg Sauce:
In a medium saucepan, melt butter or margarine. Blend in flour, salt and paprika. Add half-and-half. Stir constantly over medium-high heat until mixture thickens and bubbles. Stir in shrimp and sherry. Keep warm. Makes about 1-3/4 cups sauce.

Seafood

Here are buying tips to help you plan a seafood brunch. Listed below are amounts for an average main dish serving. If you serve seafood with a hearty sauce or as an appetizer, you'll need less.

Type of Seafood	Amount Per Serving
Fish fillets, steaks or portions	5 ounces
Clams, in-shells as an appetizer	6
Clams, shucked	1/2 to 3/4 cup
Crab meat	4 ounces
Lobster meat	4 ounces
Oysters, in shells as an appetizer	6
Oysters, shucked	1/2 to 3/4 cup
Scallops	4 to 5 ounces
Shrimp in shells	6 large
Shrimp, shelled	4 ounces

Wrap fresh fish or shellfish tightly in freezer wrap, heavy-duty foil, or heavy-weight plastic freezer bags. Fish can also be stored in airtight containers. Keep it in the coldest part of your refrigerator and use it within a day or two.

When you serve seafood, the finishing touches really count. Take time for some special garnishes but keep them simple. Individual plates need only one small, colorful garnish. For platter trims, use a single garnish slightly off-center, or two garnishes of unequal size, or three or four evenly spaced around the platter.

Crab Shells Imperial is a recipe you'll use many times. Start with large pasta shells. Stuff them with a glorious mixture of crabmeat and mushrooms and top the whole thing with a rich cheese-flavored sauce. The recipe is on page 8.

This section boasts several recipes with memorable sauces that don't have to go with a special recipe. Fresh Zucchini Sauce tastes just as marvelous over a juicy hamburger patty as it does over the Salmon Brunch Squares. Creamy Shrimp & Crab Sauce could be ladled over broiled fish fillets instead of cooked with the Pompano en Papillote, and Creamy Caper Dressing from the Seafood Salad Mold is delicious on a green salad.

Easy Seafood Newburg

An elegante entre'e laced with sherry.

4 tablespoons butter or margarine
1/4 cup all-purpose flour
1/2 teaspoon salt
1/2 teaspoon paprika
3 cups half-and-half

2 cups cooked lump crabmeat, lobster or shrimp
1/4 cup dry sherry
4 frozen patty shells, baked

In a medium saucepan, melt butter or margarine. Blend in flour, salt and paprika. Add half-and-half. Stir constantly over medium-high heat until mixture thickens and bubbles. Stir in seafood and sherry. Cook until heated through. Serve in baked patty shells. Makes 4 servings.

Paella Salad

Too hot to cook? Assemble this early in the morning using leftovers and a few gourmet shop items.

1 cup regular rice
1 teaspoon crushed saffron
Chicken broth
1/2 cup clear French or Italian salad dressing
   with herbs, more if needed
1 cup cooked peas
2 tomatoes, peeled, seeded, chopped
1/4 cup chopped green pepper
1/4 cup sliced green onion

1 (6-oz.) can lobster, drained,
   broken in chunks
1 (4-1/2-oz.) can shrimp or minced clams,
   drained
1 cup cubed cooked chicken
4 oz. smoked sausage, sliced
Lettuce
Tomato wedges

In a medium saucepan, mix rice and saffron. Substitute chicken broth for the amount of water called for on the rice package. Bring rice mixture to a boil. Reduce heat. Cover and simmer over low heat 25 minutes or until broth is absorbed. Stir in salad dressing. Refrigerate 2 hours. Fold in peas, chopped tomatoes, green pepper and green onion. Fold in lobster, shrimp or clams, chicken and sausage. Moisten with more salad dressing, if necessary. Chill. To serve, line 6 salad plates with lettuce. Serve paella on lettuce-lined plates. Garnish with tomato wedges. Makes 6 servings.

Tuna Salad Bake

Salmon fanciers may want to substitute canned salmon for the tuna fish.

2 (6-1/2-oz.) cans tuna, drained,
   broken in chunks
1 cup chopped celery
1 cup chopped fresh pears
1/2 cup toasted pecan halves

1/4 cup chopped onion
1 cup shredded Cheddar cheese (4 oz.)
3/4 cup mayonnaise or salad dressing
2 tablespoons lemon juice
2 cups crushed potato chips

Preheat oven to 425°F (220°C). In an 11" x 7" baking dish, combine tuna, celery, pears, pecans and onion. In a small bowl, fold together cheese, mayonnaise or salad dressing and lemon juice. Fold cheese mixture into tuna mixture. Top with potato chips. Bake 20 minutes or until heated through. Makes 6 servings.

Seafood is at its best when it is freshest—buy seafood from a reputable dealer and avoid seafood with a fishy odor.

Seafood Salad Mold

You'll find this tart gelatin ring mold is just right for the rich shrimp and crabmeat filling.

2 (3-oz.) pkgs. lime-flavored gelatin
2 cups boiling water
1-1/2 cups cold water
2 tablespoons lemon juice
2 cups coarsely chopped iceberg lettuce
1/4 cup sliced green onion
1/4 cup chopped celery
2 tablespoons sliced pimiento-stuffed
  green olives

Creamy Caper Dressing, see below
Lettuce
1 lb. cooked shrimp, peeled, deveined
1 cup cooked lump crabmeat
1 (14-oz.) can artichoke hearts, drained
2 Hard-Cooked Eggs, page 74, sliced

Creamy Caper Dressing:
1/2 cup mayonnaise or salad dressing
1/2 cup dairy sour cream
2 teaspoons lemon juice
2 teaspoons Dijon-style mustard
1 teaspoon Worcestershire sauce

3 tablespoons finely chopped celery
2 tablespoons drained capers
2 tablespoons chopped pimiento
1 tablespoon snipped parsley
1 Hard-Cooked Egg, page 74, chopped

Oil a 5-1/2-cup ring mold. In a large bowl, mix gelatin and 2 cups boiling water. Stir until gelatin dissolves. Stir in cold water and lemon juice. Refrigerate until partially set. Fold in lettuce, green onion, celery and olives. Turn into the oiled ring mold. Refrigerate until firm. Prepare Creamy Caper Dressing. To serve, line a plate with lettuce leaves. Unmold gelatin on the lettuce-lined plate. Fill center of gelatin ring with shrimp, crabmeat, artichokes and Hard-Cooked Eggs. Drizzle with Creamy Caper Dressing. Makes 8 servings.

Creamy Caper Dressing:
In a medium bowl, mix mayonnaise or salad dressing, sour cream, lemon juice, mustard, Worcestershire sauce, celery, capers, pimiento, parsley and chopped egg. Refrigerate until serving time. Makes 1-1/2 cups of dressing.

Easy does it! Use care when cooking fish—never overcook. The succulent flesh is done when it becomes opaque and barely flakes with a fork.

Creamy Tuna Lasagna

Best made a day ahead. But if you bake it immediately, subtract 10 minutes from the cooking time.

8 oz. lasagna noodles
Boiling salted water
2 tablespoons butter or margarine
1/2 cup chopped onion
1/2 cup chopped green pepper
2 tablespoons all-purpose flour
1 (10-1/2-oz.) can cream of chicken soup
1 cup water
1 teaspoon dried thyme

1 (8-oz.) carton dairy sour cream
2 eggs
2 (3-oz.) pkgs. cream cheese with chives,
    softened
1-1/2 cups cream-style cottage cheese (12 oz.)
1/2 cup sliced green olives
2 (6-1/2-oz.) cans tuna, well drained,
    broken in chunks
8 Hard-Cooked Eggs, page 74, sliced

Cook noodles in boiling salted water according to package directions. Drain and rinse in cold water; set aside. In a medium saucepan, melt butter or margarine. Add onion and green pepper. Cook over medium-high heat until tender, stirring occasionally. Blend in flour. Stir in soup, 1 cup water and thyme. Stir constantly over medium-high heat until mixture thickens and bubbles. Stir a small amount of hot mixture into sour cream. Add sour cream mixture to hot mixture; blend well. Remove from heat and set aside. In a medium bowl, beat eggs and cream cheese with electric mixer on high speed until fluffy. Beat in cottage cheese until combined. Fold in olives. In an ungreased 13" x 9" baking dish, layer first half the noodles, then half the cheese mixture, half the tuna, all the sliced eggs and half the soup mixture. Repeat with remaining ingredients. Cover. Refrigerate overnight. Preheat oven to 375°F (190°C). Remove lasagna from refrigerator. Uncover and bake 1 hour or until set and heated through. Let stand 15 minutes before serving. Makes 8 to 10 servings.

Salmon & Deviled Egg Bake

Devilishly good and easy enough to prepare an hour before your guests arrive.

6 Hard-Cooked Eggs, page 74
1/4 cup mayonnaise or salad dressing
1 teaspoon lemon juice
1 teaspoon prepared mustard
1/8 teaspoon salt
Dash pepper
2 tablespoons butter or margarine
2 tablespoons all-purpose flour

1 (10-oz.) pkg. frozen Welsh rarebit, thawed
1 cup milk
1 (16-oz.) can red salmon, drained,
    boned, flaked
1 (4-oz.) jar pimiento, drained, chopped
2 tablespoons snipped parsley
6 English muffins, split, buttered, toasted

Preheat oven to 375°F (190°C). Cut hard-cooked eggs in half lengthwise. Place yolks in a small bowl and mash thoroughly with a fork. Stir in mayonnaise or salad dressing, lemon juice, mustard, salt and pepper. Using a spoon, fill egg whites with yolk mixture. Place filled eggs in an 11" x 7" baking dish; set aside. In a large saucepan, melt butter or margarine. Blend in flour. Add Welsh rarebit and milk. Stir constantly over medium heat until mixture thickens and bubbles. Stir in salmon, pimiento and parsley. Pour over eggs in baking dish. Bake 30 minutes or until heated through. Serve over muffin halves. Makes 6 servings.

Stuffed Flounder Amandine

Flounder fillets wrapped around a delicate mushroom filling and topped with toasted almonds.

2 (6-oz.) cans sliced mushrooms, drained
1/2 cup dry white wine
2 tablespoons snipped parsley
1/2 teaspoon dried basil
1/8 teaspoon garlic powder
4 (5-oz.) fresh or thawed flounder or
    sole fillets

1/2 cup butter or margarine
2 tablespoons dry white wine
2 tablespoons lemon juice
1 cup sliced almonds, page 141

Preheat oven to 400°F (205°C). In a medium saucepan, mix mushrooms, 1/2 cup wine, parsley, basil and garlic powder. Cook over medium heat until most of the wine has evaporated, stirring occasionally. Spread about 1/3 cup mushroom mixture over each fillet. Roll up and tie with string. Place in an 11" x 7" baking dish. In a small saucepan, melt butter or margarine. Stir in 2 tablespoons wine and lemon juice. Pour mixture over rolled fillets in baking dish. Bake 20 minutes or only until fish barely flakes with a fork. Remove string. Top fish with toasted almonds. Makes 4 servings.

Pompano en Papillote

Spoon shrimp and crabmeat sauce over poached fillets and bake in parchment squares.

2 cups water
1 cup dry white wine
1/2 teaspoon garlic salt
2 lemon slices
1 bay leaf

5 (6-oz.) fresh or thawed frozen pompano or
    haddock fillets
Vegetable oil
Creamy Shrimp & Crab Sauce, see below

Creamy Shrimp & Crab Sauce:
2 tablespoons butter or margarine
2 tablespoons all-purpose flour
1/4 teaspoon salt
1/4 teaspoon paprika

1-1/2 cups half-and-half
1 cup shelled cooked shrimp
1 cup cooked crabmeat
1 (3-oz.) can sliced mushrooms, drained

In a large skillet, mix water, wine, garlic salt, lemon and bay leaf. Bring to a boil. Add fish. Reduce heat. Cover and simmer 5 to 10 minutes or just until fish barely flakes with a fork. Drain. Cut five 10-inch squares of parchment paper. Brush oil on one side of each square. Place squares oiled side up. Place a cooked fillet on one half of each square; set aside. Prepare Creamy Shrimp & Crab Sauce. Spoon about 1/2 cup Creamy Shrimp & Crab Sauce over each fillet. Fold half of each parchment square over fillet to make a triangle, fold up edges to seal. Place packets on a baking sheet. If desired, refrigerate packets overnight. Preheat oven to 425°F (220°C). Bake 10 to 15 minutes or until heated through. Makes 5 servings.

Creamy Shrimp & Crab Sauce:
In a medium saucepan, melt butter or margarine. Blend in flour, salt and paprika. Add half-and-half. Stir constantly over medium-high heat until mixture thickens and bubbles. Stir in shrimp, crabmeat and mushrooms. Makes about 2-1/2 cups of sauce.

Mariner's Pilaf

Two seafood favorites, lobster and crab, baked in a flavorful rice mixture.

2 cups boiling water
1-1/4 cups long-grain rice
4 tablespoons butter or margarine
1/4 cup chopped shallots or green onions
1/4 teaspoon garlic salt
1 (13-3/4-oz.) can chicken broth

1/3 cup dry sherry
1 (7-1/2-oz.) can crabmeat, drained, flaked, cartilage removed
1 (6-oz.) can lobster, drained, flaked
3 tablespoons toasted sliced almonds
2 tablespoons snipped parsley

In a 2-quart casserole, pour boiling water over rice. Let stand 40 minutes; drain. Preheat oven to 350°F (175°C). In a large skillet, melt butter or margarine. Add rice and shallots or green onions. Cook over medium-low heat until most of the butter or margarine is absorbed, stirring occasionally. Return rice mixture to the casserole. Sprinkle with garlic salt. Add broth and sherry; mix well. Gently stir in crabmeat and lobster. Cover and bake 1 hour or until all liquid is absorbed. Fluff rice mixture with a fork and stir in almonds and parsley. Cover and bake 10 minutes longer. Serve immediately. Makes 6 servings.

Variations

Substitute 1 (6-1/2-ounce) can minced clams for crabmeat or lobster.

How To Make Pompano en Papillote

1/Place a poached fish fillet diagonally on half of a 10-inch square of oiled parchment paper. Ladle about 1/2 cup of Creamy Shrimp & Crab Sauce over the fillet.

2/Fold the other half of the parchment paper diagonally over the fish to make a triangular package. Fold each of the open sides over twice to seal tightly.

Salmon Brunch Squares

A lesson in elegance—top an easy casserole with a vegetable cream sauce.

3 eggs
2 cups milk
1 cup shredded Cheddar cheese (4 oz.)
1/2 cup sliced black olives
1/4 cup sliced green onion
2 tablespoons snipped parsley

2 teaspoons Worcestershire sauce
3 cups hot cooked rice
1 (16-oz.) can red salmon, drained,
   broken in chunks, boned
Paprika
Fresh Zucchini Sauce, see below

Fresh Zucchini Sauce:
4 tablespoons butter or margarine
1 cup coarsely chopped zucchini
1/4 cup sliced green onion
1/4 cup chopped pimiento
1/4 cup all-purpose flour

1/2 teaspoon salt
1/2 teaspoon seasoned salt
1/4 teaspoon pepper
1-3/4 cups milk

Preheat oven to 325°F (165°C). In a large bowl, beat eggs slightly with a fork or whisk. Stir in milk, cheese, olives, green onion, parsley and Worcestershire sauce. Mix well. Fold in rice and salmon. Pour into a 12" x 7" baking dish. Sprinkle with paprika. Bake 45 minutes or until a knife inserted in center comes out clean. Let casserole set 10 minutes before serving. Prepare Fresh Zucchini Sauce. Cut casserole into squares and serve with Fresh Zucchini Sauce. Makes 10 servings.

Fresh Zucchini Sauce:
In a medium saucepan, melt butter or margarine. Add zucchini, green onion and pimiento. Cook over medium-high heat until zucchini is barely tender, stirring occasionally. Blend in flour, salt, seasoned salt and pepper; mix well. Add milk. Stir constantly over medium-high heat until mixture thickens and bubbles. Makes 2-1/2 cups of sauce.

Curry en Coquilles

Coquilles are shell-shaped baking dishes but any individual baking dish will do.

1-1/4 cups water
1/2 cup wild rice
1 teaspoon butter or margarine
1/2 teaspoon salt
1 lb. cooked lump crabmeat or
   cooked scallops, cut up

1-1/2 cups mayonnaise or salad dressing
2 tablespoons Dijon-style mustard
1 to 2 tablespoons curry powder
2 teaspoons lemon juice
1/3 cup grated Parmesan cheese
Paprika

In a medium saucepan, mix water, wild rice, butter or margarine and salt. Bring to a boil. Reduce heat. Cover and simmer 50 minutes or until tender. Preheat oven to 425°F (220°C). Spoon rice into 6 baking shells or ramekins. Top with crabmeat or scallops. In a small bowl, mix mayonnaise or salad dressing, mustard, curry powder and lemon juice. Spoon mixture over crabmeat or scallops. Sprinkle with cheese and paprika. Place shells on a baking sheet. Bake 15 minutes or until heated through. Makes 6 servings.

Waffles, Crepes & Pancakes

Pancakes, waffles and crepes are basically quick breads and the batters are similar. They differ in their textures and thickness and in the ways they are served.

Pancakes are round, flat, substantial cakes cooked on a griddle. They are usually topped with butter and syrup or fruit. They can be served with meats such as ham, bacon or sausage. A puffed pancake like the German Pancake on page 7, is a variation on this theme.

Waffles are crisper than pancakes. They are square with regular grooves or pockets which hold the syrup, fruit topping or sauce. They are cooked in a special electrical appliance called a *waffle iron*. There are a number of satisfactory electric waffle irons available.

Belgian Waffles are thicker and crisper than regular waffles and have extra-deep grooves or pockets. They are made with a special waffle iron. Electric Belgian waffle irons are now available but the stove-top type makes just as elegant waffles.

You can create lucious desserts with Belgian waffles, using them like a shortcake—covered with fresh fruit and topped with whipped cream or ice cream.

Crepes are very thin, delicate pancakes that are usually filled and rolled or folded.

After combining the ingredients for the crepe batter, cover and chill the mixture for 2 to 3 hours. Letting the batter stand lets the flour expand and some of the bubbles collapse. The batter will usually be smooth after it stands. If you still find lumps, strain the batter through a sieve. Thinner batters seem to work best with most crepe pans. If the batter thickens, stir in a tablespoon of milk or water.

Place a piece of waxed paper between each finished crepe so they will separate easily and stay pliable for rolling. Then cover them with a large lid or inverted bowl while you make the rest.

A large warming tray keeps toppings hot while you cook the pancakes and waffles. In addition to the sauces in this section, offer honey, fruit-flavored syrups, sweetened whipped cream and ice cream. And do try the special Fruit Butter.

Consider a pancake and waffle buffet for your next brunch. Offer a couple of variations of pancakes and waffles, with one meat sauce and one sweet topping for each. You can prepare the pancake batters ahead, then cover and refrigerate until needed. Have the waffle makings organized and the dry ingredients combined ahead of time. Because airy egg whites are included, waffle batters should not be put together too far in advance. You can do that while the waffle iron is heating.

Orange Sunshine Waffles

Maple syrup is the secret ingredient in the waffles.

1/2 cup sugar
1/4 cup cornstarch
1-3/4 cups orange juice
1/4 cup maple-flavored syrup
4 oranges, peeled, sectioned
1 (4-oz.) carton frozen whipped topping,
   thawed

1 (8-oz.) carton plain yogurt
1/4 cup maple-flavored syrup
Basic Belgian Waffles, page 119
Toasted slivered almonds, page 141

In a medium saucepan, mix sugar and cornstarch. Stir in orange juice and 1/4 cup maple syrup. Stir constantly over medium-high heat until mixture thickens and bubbles. Stir in orange sections. Cool only until warm. In a small bowl, beat whipped topping, yogurt and 1/4 cup maple syrup until fluffy. Chill until serving time. Prepare Basic Belgian Waffles. Serve waffles topped with whipped topping mixture and warm orange sauce. Garnish with toasted slivered almonds. Makes 10 servings.

Apple-Crisp Belgian Waffles

Imaginative snackers will use any leftover apple mixture as a sundae topping.

6 cups apples, peeled, cored, sliced
   (6 to 8 apples)
1-1/2 cups apple cider
1 cup brown sugar, firmly packed
1/4 cup golden raisins
1 teaspoon ground cinnamon
1/2 teaspoon ground nutmeg

1/4 cup apple cider
1/4 cup brandy or apple cider
1/4 cup all-purpose flour
3 tablespoons butter or margarine
Crunch Topping, see below
Basic Belgian Waffles, page 119
Vanilla ice cream

Crunch Topping:
4 tablespoons butter or margarine
1/2 cup quick oats

1/4 cup brown sugar, firmly packed
1/4 cup chopped pecans

In a medium saucepan, mix apples, 1-1/2 cups cider, brown sugar, raisins, cinnamon and nutmeg. Bring to a boil. Reduce heat. Cover and simmer 15 to 20 minutes or until apples are tender. In a 1-cup measure, combine 1/4 cup apple cider, 1/4 cup brandy or apple cider and flour; mix well. Stir flour mixture into apple mixture. Stir constantly over medium-high heat until mixture thickens and bubbles. Stir in 3 tablespoons butter or margarine. Keep apple mixture warm over low heat while preparing Crunch Topping and Belgian Waffles. Place a scoop of vanilla ice cream on each waffle. Pour apple mixture over ice cream and sprinkle with Crunch Topping. Makes 6 servings.

Crunch Topping:
In a small skillet, melt butter or margarine. Stir in oats, brown sugar and pecans. Stir constantly over medium-high heat until mixture is brown and crumbly.

Banana-Split Belgian Waffles

You make the first one to show how it's done—then let your guests assemble their own.

1 (6-oz.) pkg. butterscotch chips
1/2 (5.3-oz.) can evaporated milk (1/3 cup)
12 large marshmallows
Basic Belgian Waffles, page 119
2 (8-oz.) cartons strawberry yogurt

1-1/2 cups sliced bananas
2 (8-oz.) cartons banana yogurt
1-1/2 cups sliced strawberries or 1 (10-oz.)
    pkg. frozen sliced strawberries, thawed
Chopped nuts

In a small saucepan, mix butterscotch chips, evaporated milk and marshmallows. Stir constantly over low heat until mixture is melted and smooth; set aside. Prepare Belgian Waffles. Place 1 waffle square, or 1/4 waffle, on a plate. Spoon 1/4 cup strawberry yogurt and about 2 tablespoons sliced bananas on top of waffle. Cover with another waffle square, then add 1/4 cup banana yogurt and about 2 tablespoons sliced strawberries. Place a third waffle on top of the strawberries. Top with about 2 tablespoons sliced bananas and 2 tablespoons sliced strawberries. Drizzle with 3 tablespoons butterscotch sauce and sprinkle with chopped nuts. Repeat stacking process with remaining ingredients to make 5 more Banana Split Waffles. Makes 6 servings.

How To Make Banana-Split Belgian Waffles

1/Belgian waffles are made in a special waffle iron, generally of the non-electric variety although electric ones are available. Four waffle squares are made at one time. Belgian waffles have deep impressions baked into the batter to contain the fillings and sauces.

2/Stack the waffle squares, alternating the yogurt and fruit fillings. Top the third waffle with both sliced strawberries and sliced bananas. Pour the butterscotch sauce over the stack and sprinkle with chopped nuts.

Basic Belgian Waffles

Bake these extra-thick and crisp waffles on a special Belgian waffle iron.

2 cups all-purpose flour

1 teaspoon salt

8 eggs, separated

1/2 cup butter or margarine, melted

1 teaspoon vanilla extract

2 cups milk

In a small bowl, mix flour and salt; set aside. In a large bowl, beat egg whites with electric mixer on high speed until stiff peaks form. In another large bowl, beat egg yolks with electric mixer on high speed until thickened and lemon-colored, about 5 minutes. Stir in melted butter or margarine and vanilla. Alternately add flour mixture and milk to yolk mixture, beating well after each addition. Fold egg whites into yolk mixture. Prepare Belgian waffle iron according to manufacturer's directions. Using 1-1/4 cups batter for each waffle, bake on preheated waffle iron 30 to 60 seconds. Turn waffle iron; continue baking 2 to 3 minutes or until steaming stops and waffle is golden brown. Makes 6 waffles.

Wonderful Waffles

Good news if you love waffles—one basic recipe with five tempting variations.

1-3/4 cups all-purpose flour

2 tablespoons sugar

4 teaspoons baking powder

1/2 teaspoon salt

3 egg yolks, slightly beaten

1-1/2 cups milk

1/3 cup vegetable oil

3 egg whites

In a medium bowl, mix flour, sugar, baking powder and salt. In another medium bowl, mix egg yolks, milk and oil; stir into flour mixture. In a small bowl, beat egg whites with electric mixer on high speed until stiff peaks form. Fold egg whites into batter. Prepare waffle iron according to manufacturer's directions. Using 1/2 cup batter for each waffle, bake on preheated waffle iron until steaming stops and waffle is golden brown. Makes 9 waffles.

Variations

Blueberry Waffles: Sprinkle 2 tablespoons fresh or thawed frozen blueberries over waffle batter in waffle iron before baking. Serve with blueberry syrup.

Coconut-Pecan Waffles: Stir 1 cup chopped pecans and 1/2 cup flaked coconut into flour mixture with egg yolk mixture. Serve with warm honey and fruit.

Cheese Waffles: Stir 1 cup shredded process American cheese (4 ounces) into flour mixture with egg yolk mixture. Serve with sausage and taco sauce or maple syrup.

Bacon-Mushroom Waffles: Drain 1 (2-1/2-ounce) jar sliced mushrooms. Stir mushrooms into flour mixture with egg yolk mixture. Cross 2 slices cooked bacon on each waffle in waffle iron before baking. Serve with Fresh Zucchini Sauce, page 114.

Ham Waffles: Stir 1 cup fully cooked ground ham into flour mixture with egg yolk mixture. Serve with Cheddar Cheese Sauce, page 53.

Plum-Good Belgian Waffles

There's simply no other way to describe these sumptuous waffles.

3/4 cup granulated sugar
1 tablespoon cornstarch
3 cups plums, pitted, sliced (about 1-1/2 lbs.)
1/4 cup fruit-flavored wine
1 teaspoon grated lemon peel
1 tablespoon lemon juice
1/4 teaspoon ground cloves

1-1/2 cups plums, pitted and sliced
  (about 1/2 lb.)
1 (4-oz.) carton whipped cream cheese
1/4 cup powdered sugar
1 cup whipping cream,
Basic Belgian Waffles, page 119

In a medium saucepan, mix granulated sugar and cornstarch. Add 3 cups plums, wine, lemon peel, lemon juice and cloves; mix well. Bring to a boil. Reduce heat. Cover and simmer 10 minutes. Stir in 1-1/2 cups plums. Cool until just warm. In a medium bowl, beat cream cheese and powdered sugar with electric mixer on high speed until fluffy. Gradually pour in whipping cream, beating with electric mixer on high speed only until fluffy. Refrigerate until serving time. Prepare Belgian Waffles. Serve 2 waffle squares, or half a waffle, topped with about 3 tablespoons cream cheese mixture and about 1/3 cup warm plum sauce. Makes 10 servings.

Sausage & Egg Crepe Cups

Ruffled crepe cups with a hearty filling are not only pretty, but satisfying.

Basic Crepes, page 121
8 oz. bulk pork sausage
1/2 cup chopped green pepper
1/2 cup chopped onion
1/4 cup chopped pimiento

8 eggs
1/4 cup milk
1 teaspoon celery salt
Dairy sour cream
Snipped chives

Preheat oven to 375°F (190°C). Grease muffin pan cups; set aside. Prepare crepes according to recipe directions using about 1-1/2 tablespoons batter to make each 5-inch crepe. Gently place 1 crepe in each greased muffin pan cup. Arrange edges of each crepe to resemble a ruffle. In a medium skillet, combine sausage, green pepper, onion, and pimiento. Cook over medium-high heat until sausage is browned, stirring occasionally; drain. In a medium bowl, mix eggs, milk and celery salt only until combined. Sprinkle about 3 tablespoons sausage mixture into the bottom of each crepe cup. Pour about 3 tablespoons egg mixture over sausage mixture. Bake 25 to 30 minutes or until a knife inserted in center of a cup comes out clean. Let stand 5 minutes; remove from pan. Top with a dollop of sour cream and sprinkle with chives. Serve immediately. Makes 6 servings.

Be sure to lightly oil your waffle maker each time before using to prevent waffles from sticking.

Basic Crepes

Stack these paper-thin pancakes between waxed paper, then wrap in a plastic bag and freeze.

4 eggs
2-1/3 cups milk
2 cups all-purpose flour

3 tablespoons vegetable oil
1/4 teaspoon salt

In a large bowl, beat eggs with electric mixer on medium speed until well combined. Add milk, flour, oil and salt. Beat with electric mixer on medium speed until batter is smooth. Cover and refrigerate 2 to 3 hours. Prepare crepe pan according to manufacturer's directions or preheat a small, shallow skillet; brush with oil if pan does not have a non-stick finish. Using about 2 tablespoons batter for each crepe, cook on preheated crepe pan over medium-high heat 2 to 3 minutes or until underside is lightly browned. To remove, loosen edges and gently lift crepe with spatula. Stack crepes between squares of waxed paper for easy separation. Makes about 30 crepes.

Chicken Divan Crepes

The filling for this perfect brunch dish is simplified with canned soup.

8 Basic Crepes, above
1 (10-1/2-oz.) can condensed
   cream of chicken soup
1 cup shredded sharp Cheddar cheese (4 oz.)
1/3 cup mayonnaise or salad dressing
1 teaspoon curry powder
1 teaspoon lemon juice

2 cups cubed cooked chicken
1 (10-oz.) pkg. frozen chopped broccoli,
   cooked, drained
1 (2-1/2-oz.) jar sliced mushrooms, drained
Grated Parmesan cheese
Paprika

Prepare crepes; set aside. Preheat oven to 375°F (190°C). In a medium saucepan, mix soup and Cheddar cheese. Stir constantly over low heat until cheese melts. Stir in mayonnaise or salad dressing, curry powder and lemon juice. Add chicken, broccoli and mushrooms; mix well. Spoon about 1/2 cup chicken mixture onto center of each crepe. Roll up and place in a 13" x 9" baking dish. Cover and bake 20 to 25 minutes or until heated through. Sprinkle with Parmesan cheese and paprika. Serve immediately. Makes 4 servings.

Freeze leftover waffles in moisture-proof wrap. To serve, unwrap and reheat them in the toaster.

Asparagus Cordon Bleu Crepes

Tarragon's flavor resembles anise or licorice and it enhances vegetables and cream sauces.

8 Basic Crepes, page 121
1-1/2 lbs. fresh asparagus spears
Boiling salted water
8 thin slices cooked ham
Dijon-style mustard
8 slices Swiss cheese
2 tomatoes, peeled, seeded, chopped
Snipped parsley

Crushed dried tarragon, as desired
3 tablespoons butter or margarine
3 tablespoons all-purpose flour
1/2 teaspoon dried tarragon, crushed
1/2 teaspoon salt
Dash pepper
1-1/2 cups half-and-half
1 (2-1/2-oz.) jar sliced mushrooms, drained

Prepare crepes; set aside. Preheat oven to 375°F (190°C). Trim asparagus spears. In a large sauce-pan, cook asparagus spears in boiling salted water until crisp-tender; drain. Place a slice of ham on each crepe. Spread ham slice with mustard. Top with a slice of cheese, asparagus spears and toma-toes. Sprinkle with parsley and tarragon, as desired. Roll up crepes. In a 13" x 9" baking dish, place crepes seam-side down. In a medium saucepan, melt butter or margarine. Blend in flour, 1/2 tea-spoon dried tarragon, salt and pepper. Stir in half-and-half. Stir constantly over medium-high heat until mixture thickens and bubbles. Stir in mushrooms. Pour sauce over crepes in baking dish. Bake 25 minutes or until heated through. Makes 4 to 6 servings.

Haystack Chocolate Pancakes

Scrumptious coconut-pecan sauce poured on airy chocolate pancakes that start with a mix.

Coconut-Pecan Topping, see below
2 cups pancake mix
1/2 cup unsweetened cocoa powder

Milk
Eggs
Vegetable oil

Coconut-Pecan Topping:
1 (13-oz.) can evaporated milk
1 cup sugar
3 egg yolks
1/2 cup butter or margarine

1 teaspoon vanilla extract
1 cup flaked coconut
1/2 cup chopped pecans

Prepare Coconut-Pecan Topping; keep warm. In a large bowl, thoroughly combine pancake mix and cocoa. Prepare pancakes with milk, eggs and vegetable oil according to package directions for 2 cups of mix. Preheat griddle. Brush preheated griddle with oil. Using scant 1/4 cup batter for each pan-cake, cook over medium-high heat 2 to 3 minutes or until underside is browned and surface is bubbly. Turn and cook 1 to 2 minutes or until other side is browned. Serve with warm Coconut-Pecan Topping. Makes 16 to 18 servings.

Coconut-Pecan Topping:
In a medium saucepan, mix evaporated milk, sugar, egg yolks, butter or margarine and vanilla. Stir constantly over medium heat until thickened. Stir in coconut and pecans. Makes 3 cups of topping.

Piña Colada Pancakes

Airy pineapple-coconut pancakes with rum sauce—delicious!

Fluffy Rum Sauce, page 125
2 cups all-purpose flour
2 tablespoons baking powder
1/4 cup sugar
1/2 teaspoon salt
1 (15-1/4-oz.) can crushed pineapple

2 eggs, beaten
1 cup milk
1/4 cup vegetable oil
1 cup flaked coconut
Additional coconut, if desired
Pineapple rings, if desired

Prepare Fluffy Rum Sauce; refrigerate until serving time. In a large bowl, mix flour, baking powder, sugar and salt. Drain crushed pineapple, reserving syrup. Add water to syrup to make 1 cup liquid. In a medium bowl, combine eggs, syrup-water mixture, milk and vegetable oil. Add to flour mixture. Stir only until combined; the batter will still be lumpy. In a small bowl, mix drained pineapple and coconut. Preheat griddle. Brush preheated griddle with oil. Using 1/4 cup batter for each pancake, pour batter onto griddle. Sprinkle each pancake with 1 tablespoon pineapple mixture. Cook over medium-high heat 2 to 3 minutes or until underside is golden brown and surface is bubbly. Turn and cook 2 to 3 minutes more or until other side is golden brown. Serve with Fluffy Rum Sauce, additional coconut and halved pineapple rings, if desired. Makes 16 pancakes.

How To Make Piña Colada Pancakes

1/Pour 1/4 cup batter for each pancake on a preheated griddle. Sprinkle with a spoonful of the pineapple-coconut mixture. Cook until bubbles form on top of pancakes. Turn and cook the other side until golden brown.

2/Top pancakes with pineapple rings and shredded coconut. Ladle Fluffy Rum Sauce over pancakes and serve piping hot.

Fluffy Rum Sauce

This is the perfect topping for Piña Colada Pancakes, page 124.

4 egg yolks
1-1/2 cups powdered sugar

1/4 cup rum
2 tablespoons frozen whipped topping, thawed

In a medium bowl, beat egg yolks with electric mixer on high speed until thickened and lemon-colored, about 5 minutes. Add powdered sugar and continue beating on medium speed until combined. Gradually beat in rum until blended. Fold in whipped topping. Makes about 2 cups of sauce.

Strawberry Blossom Pancakes

The strawberry topping is as easy as 1-2-3! Try it over cake slices too.

1 (16-oz.) pkg. frozen whole strawberries,
    thawed
Strawberry Fluff, see below
2 cups all-purpose flour
1/4 cup sugar
2 tablespoons baking powder
1 teaspoon salt

1/2 teaspoon baking soda
2 eggs, beaten
1-1/2 cups milk
1 (8-oz.) carton dairy sour cream
2 tablespoons vegetable oil
Fresh strawberries for garnish

Strawberry Fluff:
1 (4-1/2-oz.) carton frozen whipped topping,
    thawed
1/3 cup dairy sour cream

1/4 cup reserved strawberry juice
Reserved frozen whole strawberries,
    well drained

Thoroughly drain strawberries, reserving 1/4 cup juice for topping. Chop 1/2 cup drained strawberries; reserve remainder for topping. Prepare Strawberry Fluff; set aside. In a medium bowl, mix flour, sugar, baking powder, salt and baking soda. In another medium bowl, mix eggs, milk, sour cream and oil. Add to flour mixture. Add 1/2 cup chopped strawberries. Stir only until combined; the batter will still be lumpy. Preheat griddle. Brush preheated griddle with oil. Using 1/4 cup batter for each pancake, cook over medium-high heat 2 to 3 minutes or until underside is golden brown and surface is bubbly. Turn and cook 2 to 3 minutes more or until other side is golden brown. Keep warm. Spread 1 pancake with about 1/3 cup Strawberry Fluff; repeat with 7 more pancakes. Top with remaining pancakes. Garnish with an additional dollop of Strawberry Fluff and a fresh strawberry. Makes 8 servings.

Strawberry Fluff:
In medium bowl, whisk together whipped topping, sour cream, and 1/4 cup reserved strawberry juice. Fold in reserved well-drained whole strawberries. Makes 3-1/2 cups of topping.

Peach Melba Pancakes

When it comes to flavor, this is a sensation! Try the sauce drizzled over peach ice cream.

Regal Raspberry Sauce, see below
1 cup all-purpose flour
1 tablespoon sugar
1 tablespoon baking powder
1/4 teaspoon salt
1/4 teaspoon baking soda

1 (16-oz.) can sliced peaches
1 egg, beaten
1/2 cup milk
1/2 (8-oz.) carton peach-flavored yogurt
2 tablespoons vegetable oil

Regal Raspberry Sauce:
1 (10-oz.) pkg. frozen raspberries, thawed
1 tablespoon sugar

1 tablespoon cornstarch
1/3 cup currant jelly

Prepare Regal Raspberry Sauce; set aside. In a large bowl, mix flour, sugar, baking powder, salt and baking soda. Drain peach slices, reserving 1/4 cup syrup. In a medium bowl, mix egg, milk, reserved peach syrup, yogurt and vegetable oil. Add to flour mixture. Stir only until combined; the batter will still be lumpy. Preheat griddle. Brush preheated griddle with oil. Using 1/4 cup batter for each pancake, cook over medium-high heat 2 to 3 minutes or until underside is golden brown and surface is bubbly. Turn and cook 2 to 3 minutes more or until other side is golden brown. Keep warm. Top with drained peach slices and drizzle with Regal Raspberry Sauce. Makes 8 pancakes.

Regal Raspberry Sauce:
Press raspberries through a sieve; discard seeds. Measure 3/4 cup sieved juice. In a small saucepan, combine sugar and cornstarch. Gradually stir in raspberry juice. Add currant jelly. Stir constantly over medium-high heat until thickened and bubbly. Cook 1 minute longer. Makes 1 cup of sauce.

Fresh Fruit Butter

Create a melt-in-your-mouth butter to spread on a piping hot pancake or waffle.

1/2 cup butter or margarine, softened
2 cups powdered sugar
1 egg yolk

1 cup sliced strawberries, peaches,
  plums or pears
1/3 cup ground nuts, if desired

In a small bowl, beat butter or margarine, powdered sugar and egg yolk with electric mixer on high speed until fluffy. In a food processor or blender, puree fruit. Slowly beat fruit puree into powdered sugar mixture with electric mixer on low speed; beat until smooth. Stir in nuts, if desired. Makes about 2-1/2 cups.

Beat together your favorite jam and softened butter to make a sweet topping for waffles or pancakes.

Salads & Vegetables

A savory salad or vegetable will round out your brunch menu. Although brunch will be the first meal of the day for some people, most of your guests will have had a little something to hold them over. They'll be expecting the lunch part of brunch and will appreciate discovering salads and vegetables on the table.

Would you like to serve a tossed salad, but hate the last-minute flurry it usually takes? Here are several overnight tossed salads. The day before the brunch, layer a salad in your prettiest bowl, tuck it away in the refrigerator and it will be ready to toss at brunch time. Crunchy 24-Hour Vegetable Toss with crumbled bacon and canned French fried onion rings, is easy to put together and is almost a meal by itself! Parmesan Vegetable Marinade, page 13, picks up flavor from the dressing overnight. Party Scalloped Potatoes goes together quickly but is different from any potatoes you've had before.

The recipe is on page 21.

Unmolding gelatin salads can be a frustrating experience. For best results, oil the mold lightly before filling it. To unmold, dip the mold up to the rim in hot water for a few seconds. Then use a knife to gently loosen the first inch or so around the top of the mold. Place a wet platter upside-down over the mold. Quickly invert the platter and mold so the platter is right-side up. The mold should slip right out. If the mold is stubborn, repeat the quick dip in hot water and, with a table knife or small spatula, work down the side of the mold in one spot to relieve the suction. Then invert and try again. The wet platter will allow you to move the mold on the plate if necessary.

Some sweet salads can double as dessert. This can be especially convenient if your guests are light eaters and want to end the meal with something sweet without feeling stuffed.

Overnight Orange Toss

Layer fruit and vegetables, and seal in the flavors with a tangy yogurt dressing.

12 cups torn mixed greens
2 medium oranges, peeled, sectioned
1 avocado, peeled, seeded, sliced
Ascorbic acid color keeper
1/2 medium cucumber, peeled, seeded, sliced
1 small red onion, sliced, separated into rings

1/2 cup chopped green pepper
2 cups shredded Monterey Jack cheese (8 oz.)
1/2 cup orange yogurt
1/2 cup creamy French salad dressing
1 teaspoon celery seeds
1/4 cup toasted slivered almonds, page 141

In a large salad bowl, layer half the greens. Add orange sections. Treat avocado with ascorbic acid color keeper according to package directions. Layer avocado over orange sections. Layer first the cucumber, then onion, green pepper and finally the cheese. Top salad with remaining greens. In a small bowl, mix yogurt, salad dressing and celery seeds. Spread yogurt mixture over the top of the salad, sealing to edges of the bowl. Top with almonds. Refrigerate up to 24 hours. Toss before serving. Makes 12 servings.

World's Greatest Hot Spinach Salad

Superb dressing drizzled over spinach, hard-cooked eggs and chopped radishes.

1 (10-oz.) pkg. fresh spinach, washed,
   torn in bite-size pieces
4 Hard-Cooked Eggs, page 74, sliced
2 tablespoons chopped radishes
8 slices bacon
1/4 cup sliced green onion

4 teaspoons all-purpose flour
1/2 teaspoon celery salt
1/2 cup water
3 tablespoons lemon juice
1 tablespoon prepared horseradish
1 tablespoon Worcestershire sauce

Place spinach, Hard-Cooked Eggs and radishes in a salad bowl. Refrigerate until serving time. Just before serving, cook bacon in a medium skillet over medium-high heat until crisp. Drain bacon on paper towels. Reserve 1/3 cup drippings in skillet. Crumble bacon and set aside. Cook onion in reserved drippings over medium-high heat until tender, stirring occasionally. Blend in flour and celery salt. Add water, lemon juice, horseradish and Worcestershire sauce. Stir constantly over medium-high heat until mixture thickens and bubbles. Stir crumbled bacon into sauce. Pour sauce over spinach mixture and toss. Serve immediately. Makes 6 servings.

Hot Bean Salad Toss

Tangy dressing delicately coats the vegetables.

6 slices bacon
1 small red onion, sliced, separated into rings
1/4 medium green pepper, cut in strips
1 tablespoon all-purpose flour
1 tablespoon sugar
1/2 teaspoon salt
1/4 teaspoon pepper
1/2 cup water

1/4 cup red wine vinegar
4 cups torn mixed greens
1 (8-oz.) can cut green beans, drained
1 (8-oz.) can cut wax beans, drained
1 (8-oz.) can red kidney beans, drained, rinsed
1/2 cup sliced fresh mushrooms
1/4 cup pimiento strips

In a large skillet, cook bacon over medium-high heat until crisp. Drain bacon on paper towels. Reserve 1/4 cup drippings in skillet. Crumble bacon and set aside. Cook onion and green pepper in bacon drippings over medium-high heat until tender, stirring occasionally. Blend in flour, sugar, salt and pepper. Add water and vinegar. Stir constantly over medium-high heat until mixture thickens and bubbles. Remove from heat. In a large salad bowl, mix greens, green beans, wax beans, kidney beans, mushrooms and pimiento. Pour hot dressing over salad. Toss to coat all vegetables. Sprinkle with crumbled bacon. Makes 8 servings.

Crunchy 24-Hour Vegetable Toss

Escape the last minute rush by assembling this salad the day before.

1 large head iceberg lettuce, torn in
   bite-size pieces
6 Hard-Cooked Eggs, page 74, sliced
Salad seasoning
10 slices bacon, crisp-cooked,
   drained, crumbled
1 cup shredded carrot

2 cups cauliflowerets (1 head)
1/2 cup thinly sliced radishes
1 cup crumbled blue cheese (4 oz.)
2 cups shredded sharp Cheddar cheese (8 oz.)
1/2 cup mayonnaise or salad dressing
1/2 cup dairy sour cream
1 (3-oz.) can French fried onions

In a large salad bowl, layer half the lettuce. Arrange the egg slices in a layer and sprinkle with salad seasoning. Layer first the bacon, then carrot, cauliflowerets, radishes and finally the remaining lettuce. Sprinkle with more salad seasoning. Top with blue cheese, then Cheddar cheese. In a small bowl, mix mayonnaise or salad dressing and sour cream until blended. Spread over the cheese layer, sealing to edges of the bowl. Cover and refrigerate up to 24 hours. Before serving, top with French fried onions; toss. Makes 12 servings.

Deluxe Vinaigrette Salad *Photo on page 4.*

Brush avocado slices with ascorbic acid color keeper or lemon juice to keep the fresh color.

Vinaigrette Dressing, see below
2 heads Boston lettuce
1 (4-1/2-oz.) can tiny shrimp, drained
9 cherry tomatoes, halved
2 Hard-Cooked Eggs, page 74, sliced

1 avocado, peeled, seeded, sliced
Ripe olives
6 slices bacon, crisp-cooked,
   drained, crumbled
1/4 cup blue cheese, crumbled

Vinaigrette Dressing:
1/2 cup vegetable oil
1/3 cup white wine tarragon vinegar

1 envelope Italian salad dressing mix

Prepare Vinaigrette Dressing; refrigerate until serving time. Arrange Boston lettuce leaves on 6 salad plates. Arrange shrimp, cherry tomato halves, egg slices, avocado slices and olives on lettuce. Sprinkle with crumbled bacon and blue cheese. Chill. Before serving, shake dressing and drizzle over salads. Makes 6 servings.

Vinaigrette Dressing:
In a cruet or screw-top jar, mix oil, vinegar and salad dressing mix. Shake well. Makes about 1 cup.

> *Use ascorbic acid color keeper or lemon juice to maintain the color of raw cut fruits such as apples, apricots, avocados, bananas, pears or peaches.*

Marinated Potato Salad

Here's a make-ahead that's just right for summer entertaining.

4 cups cubed hot cooked potatoes
1/3 cup clear Italian salad dressing
1/4 cup chopped green onion
1/4 cup chopped celery
1/4 cup sliced pimiento-stuffed green olives

3 Hard-Cooked Eggs, page 74, sliced
1/3 cup mayonnaise or salad dressing
1 teaspoon Dijon-style mustard
1/2 teaspoon prepared horseradish
1/4 teaspoon celery seeds

In a large bowl, gently toss hot potatoes and Italian salad dressing. Chill, stirring occasionally. Add green onion, celery, olives and eggs. In a small bowl, mix mayonnaise or salad dressing, mustard, horseradish and celery seeds. Fold mayonnaise mixture into potato mixture. Refrigerate until serving time. Makes 8 servings.

Macaroni & Cheese Salad

Don't count on leftovers with this creamy salad.

2 cups tiny shell macaroni, cooked, drained
1/2 cup creamy Italian salad dressing
1/4 cup chopped onion
1/4 cup chopped green pepper
1/4 cup chopped pimiento

1/4 cup chopped celery
1/4 cup shredded carrot
2 cups shredded sharp Cheddar cheese (8 oz.)
1/2 cup mayonnaise or salad dressing
1 teaspoon prepared mustard

In a large bowl, combine hot macaroni and Italian salad dressing; mix well. Add onion, green pepper, pimiento, celery and carrot; toss to mix well. Chill. Toss cheese with chilled macaroni mixture. In a small bowl, mix mayonnaise or salad dressing and mustard. Fold into macaroni mixture. Refrigerate until serving time. Makes 8 servings.

Minted Pear Dessert Salad

A baking dish doesn't need oil. If you use a mold, it might help to oil it first.

1 (29-oz.) can pear halves in heavy syrup
1 (3-oz.) pkg. lime-flavored gelatin
1 (6-1/2-oz.) pkg. miniature marshmallows
 (3-1/2 cups)

1 (8-oz.) pkg. butter mint candies, crushed,
 firmly packed (1 cup)
1 (9-oz.) carton whipped topping, thawed
Fresh mint sprigs, if desired

Drain pear halves, reserving 1 cup syrup. Chop pears. In a large bowl, mix pears, reserved pear syrup, lime gelatin, marshmallows and mint candies. Cover and refrigerate 3 hours or until marshmallows begin to dissolve. Fold in whipped topping. Turn into a 7-cup mold or a 13" x 9" baking dish. Freeze 8 hours or overnight until firm. Garnish with fresh mint sprigs, if desired. Makes 14 servings.

Herbed Pea Salad

Vegetables are marinated in a tasty buttermilk-herb dressing.

2 (10-oz.) pkgs. frozen peas, cooked, drained
1/2 cup chopped celery
1/4 cup chopped green onion
1/4 cup chopped pimiento
1 (.4-oz.) envelope herb dressing mix
   (buttermilk-style)

1 cup mayonnaise or salad dressing
1/2 cup buttermilk
2 cups cubed cheese with peppers (8 oz.)
2 Hard-Cooked Eggs, page 74, sliced
1 cup cheese-flavored croutons or
   herbed-flavored croutons

In a large bowl, mix peas, celery, green onion and pimiento. In a small bowl, mix dressing mix, mayonnaise or salad dressing and buttermilk. Beat with a whisk until smooth. Fold dressing into vegetable mixture. Cover and refrigerate 3 hours or overnight. Just before serving, fold in cheese, eggs and croutons. Makes 8 to 10 servings.

How To Make Herbed Pea Salad

1/Use a whisk to blend the herb dressing mix with buttermilk and mayonnaise or salad dressing. Then fold the dressing into the salad.

2/After the salad has been chilled, carefully fold in the hard-cooked egg slices, cheese cubes and crisp croutons. Serve immediately.

Succotash Salad

Mixed corn and green or lima beans is the base for succotash, an American Indian dish.

1 (10-oz.) pkg. frozen whole kernel corn,
   cooked, drained
1 (9-oz.) pkg. frozen Italian green beans,
   cooked, drained
1 cup sliced fresh mushrooms
1 cup sliced celery
1/2 cup chopped pimiento

1/4 cup chopped green onion
2/3 cup creamy Italian salad dressing
1 teaspoon dried basil
1 teaspoon dried oregano
1/2 teaspoon celery salt
Lettuce leaves

In a medium bowl, mix corn and green beans. Fold in mushrooms, celery, pimiento and green onion. In a measuring cup or small bowl, mix Italian salad dressing, basil, oregano and celery salt. Pour dressing over vegetable mixture; mix gently. Cover and refrigerate 4 hours or overnight, stirring occasionally. Arrange lettuce leaves in a medium salad bowl. Spoon vegetable mixture into the lettuce-lined bowl. Makes 8 servings.

Dilled Zucchini Spears

Fresh dill can sometimes be found in specialty food shops or large supermarkets.

4 to 6 medium zucchini
1 onion, sliced, separated into rings
3 to 4 heads fresh dill or
   1 tablespoon dried dill seed
Cracked ice
1 cup white wine tarragon vinegar
1 cup water

2 tablespoons pickling salt
2 tablespoons sugar
1 teaspoon celery seeds
1 teaspoon mustard seeds
1/4 to 1/2 teaspoon hot pepper sauce
2 garlic cloves, minced

Cut zucchini in half crosswise, then cut lengthwise into sixths or eighths to form serving-size spears. In a crock or shallow baking dish, layer zucchini spears, onion, fresh dill or dill seeds and enough ice to cover. Let stand 3 hours; drain. In a small saucepan, mix vinegar, water, pickling salt, sugar, celery seeds, mustard seeds, hot pepper sauce and garlic. Stir constantly over medium-high heat only until sugar and salt dissolve. Pour vinegar mixture over the zucchini mixture. Cover and refrigerate 2 days or up to several weeks. Makes about 6 cups.

Asparagus Salad Vinaigrette

Enhance the dressing-marinade with chopped fresh vegetables and herbs.

1 (10-oz.) pkg. frozen asparagus spears,
  cooked, drained
2/3 cup herbed vinegar and oil salad dressing
3 tablespoons chopped radishes
3 tablespoons chopped green pepper
2 tablespoons dill pickle relish

1 tablespoon snipped parsley
1 tablespoon snipped chives
Fresh spinach
2 Hard-Cooked Eggs, page 74, sliced
1 tomato, cut in wedges

Place asparagus spears in a 10" x 6" baking dish. In a screw-top jar, mix salad dressing, radish, green pepper, relish, parsley and chives; shake well. Pour dressing mixture over asparagus. Cover and refrigerate 4 to 24 hours. Before serving, arrange spinach leaves on salad plates. With a slotted spoon, lift asparagus onto spinach-lined plates. Arrange egg slices and tomato wedges around asparagus. Drizzle with some of the asparagus marinade. Makes 4 servings.

Blue Cheese & Cucumber Platter

If you like the flavor of blue cheese, this will be one of your favorites.

1/2 cup crumbled blue cheese (2 oz.)
1/3 cup vegetable oil
2 tablespoons lemon juice
2 teaspoons paprika
1 teaspoon celery salt
1/4 teaspoon freshly ground pepper

1 medium onion, thinly sliced,
  separated into rings
1 large cucumber, thinly sliced
Leaf lettuce
3 large tomatoes, sliced

In a small bowl, beat blue cheese, oil, lemon juice, paprika, celery salt and pepper with electric mixer on medium speed until combined. Stir in onion and cucumber. Cover and refrigerate 8 hours or overnight. Before serving, arrange lettuce leaves on a platter. Place tomatoes on lettuce. Spoon onion-cucumber mixture over tomatoes. Makes 6 to 8 servings.

Keep salad greens at the peak of freshness and crispness! Store washed greens wrapped in paper towels in sealed plastic bags in the refrigerator for best eating quality.

Cherry-Banana Dessert Salad

Drizzling with lemon juice prevents the banana from turning brown.

2 (3-oz.) pkgs. cream cheese, softened
1 (4-1/2-oz.) carton frozen whipped topping,
    thawed
2 cups sliced bananas
1 tablespoon lemon juice

1 (21-oz.) can cherry pie filling
1/2 cup chopped pecans
Sliced bananas
Additional whipped topping
Chopped pecans

Line a 9" x 5" loaf pan or a 5-cup ring mold with foil; set aside. In a large bowl, beat cream cheese with electric mixer on medium speed until fluffy. Beat in 4-1/2 ounces whipped topping until well combined. Place 2 cups bananas in a small bowl. Drizzle with lemon juice and toss to coat all banana slices. Fold bananas, cherry pie filling and 1/2 cup chopped pecans into the cream cheese mixture. Turn into the foil-lined pan. Freeze 8 hours or overnight until firm. Remove from freezer and let stand about 20 minutes before serving. Turn out of pan, remove foil and slice. Garnish with sliced bananas, additional whipped topping and pecans. Makes 8 servings.

Strawberry Swirl Salad Squares

Dessert salads are popular now. Here's one reason why.

2 (3-oz.) pkgs. strawberry gelatin
2 cups boiling water
2 (10-oz.) pkgs. frozen sliced strawberries
    with sugar added
1/2 cup water

2 (3-oz.) pkgs. cream cheese, softened
1/4 cup milk
2 tablespoons mayonnaise or salad dressing
Lettuce leaves
Fresh strawberries, if desired

In a large bowl, dissolve gelatin in 2 cups boiling water. Add frozen strawberries. Stir to thaw strawberries, using a large fork to break up frozen berries. Stir in 1/2 cup water. Turn mixture into an ungreased 8-inch square baking dish. Refrigerate until partially set. In a small bowl, beat cream cheese and milk with electric mixer on medium speed until fluffy. Beat in mayonnaise or salad dressing. Spread cream cheese mixture on top of gelatin. Cut through cheese mixture with a knife to create a marbled effect. Refrigerate until set. Arrange lettuce leaves on salad plates. Cut salad into squares and serve on lettuce-lined plates. Garnish with fresh strawberries, if desired. Makes 9 servings.

Orange Blossom Salad

A layered salad that looks as good as it tastes.

1 (3-oz.) pkg. lemon-flavored gelatin
1-1/2 cups boiling water
1/4 cup lemon juice
1 (8-oz.) pkg. cream cheese, softened
1 cup shredded Cheddar cheese (4 oz.)
1/2 cup chopped pecans
1 (15-1/4-oz.) can pineapple chunks packed
   in its own juice

2 (3-oz.) pkgs. orange-flavored gelatin
2 cups champagne or ginger ale
2 (11-oz.) cans mandarin orange sections,
   drained
Leaf lettuce
Orange Twists, page 147
Frosted Grape Clusters, page 105

Lightly oil a 10-cup ring mold; set aside. In a small saucepan, dissolve lemon gelatin in boiling water. Stir in lemon juice. Place cream cheese in a medium bowl. Gradually add lemon gelatin mixture to cream cheese, beating with electric mixer on medium speed until smooth. Refrigerate until partially set. Fold in Cheddar cheese and pecans. Turn into the oiled mold. Refrigerate until almost firm. Drain pineapple, reserving juice. Set pineapple aside. Add water to pineapple juice to make 1-1/2 cups. In a small saucepan, bring pineapple juice mixture to a boil. Dissolve orange gelatin in boiling pineapple juice mixture. Slowly and gently stir in champagne or ginger ale. Refrigerate until partially set. Fold in orange sections and reserved pineapple chunks. Pour over cream cheese mixture in mold. Refrigerate 8 hours or overnight until firm. Before serving, arrange lettuce leaves on a platter. Unmold salad on lettuce-lined plate. Garnish with Orange Twists and Frosted Grape Clusters. Makes 12 to 14 servings.

Molded Slaw Salad

Cole slaw in a colorful mold has lots of eye appeal.

2 (3-oz.) pkgs. lemon-flavored gelatin
2 cups boiling water
1/2 cup dill pickle juice
1/4 cup cold water
2 tablespoons finely chopped onion
2 tablespoons lemon juice
1/2 teaspoon salt
1 cup mayonnaise or salad dressing

2-1/2 cups chopped cabbage
1/2 cup shredded carrot
1/2 cup chopped, seeded, peeled cucumber
1/3 cup chopped dill pickle
Leaf lettuce
Assorted relishes such as carrot sticks and
   radishes, or pickles and olives

Oil a 6-cup ring mold; set aside. In a large bowl, dissolve gelatin in 2 cups boiling water. Stir in dill pickle juice, 1/4 cup cold water, onion, lemon juice and salt; mix well. Add mayonnaise or salad dressing; beat with a whisk until smooth. Refrigerate until partially set. Fold in cabbage, carrot, cucumber and dill pickle. Pour mixture into the oiled mold. Refrigerate 6 hours or overnight until set. Before serving, arrange lettuce leaves on a platter. Unmold salad on lettuce-lined platter. Fill center of mold with assorted relishes. Makes 12 servings.

Lazy-Day Scalloped Potatoes

You may prefer to use half-and-half instead of milk in this quick and easy dish.

2 (5-1/2-oz.) pkgs. dry scalloped potato mix
6 tablespoons butter or margarine
5 cups boiling water
1-1/3 cups milk

1 (4-oz.) can whole green chilies, drained,
   seeded, chopped
1-1/2 cups shredded Cheddar cheese (6 oz.)

Preheat oven to 350°F (175°C). Place 1 package of potatoes in a 3-quart casserole. Sprinkle with the sauce mix packet. Add half the butter or margarine, half the boiling water, half the milk, half the chilies and half the cheese. Repeat with remaining ingredients. Bake uncovered 50 to 60 minutes. Makes 8 servings.

Broccoli-Cauliflower Sauté

An easy way to serve piping hot fresh vegetables—the pot-watching is done early.

1 lb. fresh broccoli (3-1/2 to 4 cups cut up)
2 cups fresh cauliflowerets
2 qts. boiling salted water

Ice water
1/3 cup butter or margarine
1/4 cup minced parsley

Wash broccoli and separate into flowerets and stems. Trim and peel stems; cut into 1-inch pieces. Drop stem pieces into 2 quarts boiling salted water. Cook 2 minutes. Add broccoli flowerets and cauliflowerets. Cook 2 minutes longer. Drain, then plunge into ice water. Remove immediately, drain well and set aside or refrigerate. To serve, melt butter or margarine in a large skillet. Add vegetables. Shake skillet and gently stir vegetables over medium heat until heated through, 2 to 3 minutes. Toss with parsley. Makes 6 to 8 servings.

Peas & Carrots Tarragon

Cook the carrots ahead and the rest is easy!

6 medium carrots
2 qts. boiling salted water
Ice water
1 (10-oz.) pkg. frozen peas, thawed

1/3 cup butter or margarine
1/4 cup sliced green onion
1/4 cup minced parsley
1/2 teaspoon dried tarragon, crushed

Scrape carrots. Remove ends and cut into matchstick pieces. Drop into boiling salted water; cook 4 minutes. Drain, then plunge into ice water. Remove immediately, drain well and set aside or refrigerate. At serving time, place peas in a sieve or colander. Run hot water over peas; drain well. Melt butter or margarine in a large skillet. Add onion. Cook until onion is partially tender. Add peas and carrots. Shake skillet and gently stir vegetables over medium heat until heated through, about 5 minutes. Toss with parsley and tarragon. Makes 6 to 8 servings.

Green Bean Sauté

Get acquainted with Jerusalem artichokes! Delightful with fresh green beans.

1 lb. fresh green beans	Lemon juice
2 qts. boiling salted water	1/3 cup butter or margarine
Ice water	1/4 cup minced parsley
1/2 lb. fresh Jerusalem artichokes	1/2 teaspoon dried oregano, crushed
Cold water	

Wash beans and remove ends and strings; cut diagonally in 1-inch pieces. Drop into boiling salted water. Cook uncovered 12 minutes. Drain well, then plunge quickly into ice water. Remove immediately, drain well and set aside or refrigerate. Scrub artichokes and peel under cold running water. Drop into a bowl of cold water with a little lemon juice added to prevent darkening. At serving time, melt butter or margarine in a large skillet. Cut artichokes into thin slices. Add artichokes and beans to skillet. Shake skillet and gently stir vegetables over medium heat until heated through, 5 to 6 minutes. Toss with parsley and oregano. Makes 6 to 8 servings.

How To Make Green Bean Sauté

1/Cook fresh green beans until barely tender, 12 minutes. Drain in a colander and plunge into a bowl of ice water to stop the cooking. Drain again before setting aside.

2/Jerusalem artichokes or *sunchokes* are knobby relatives of the sunflower. Peel off the thin outside brown covering, then drop the artichokes into a mixture of lemon juice and water to prevent them from darkening. Before serving, slice the artichokes and sauté them with the green beans.

Broiled Herbed Tomatoes

Try this with your next crop of green tomatoes.

4 large ripe tomatoes
4 tablespoons butter or margarine
1/2 cup fine dry seasoned breadcrumbs
1/4 cup grated Parmesan cheese

1/4 cup chopped onion
1 teaspoon dried savory or dried basil
Dash pepper
Dairy sour cream

Preheat broiler at moderate temperature. Cut tomatoes in half. Place on rack in broiler pan, cut sides up. In a small saucepan, melt butter or margarine. Remove from heat. Stir in breadcrumbs, Parmesan cheese, onion, savory or basil and pepper. Broil tomatoes 4 inches from heat 4 minutes. Remove from oven and sprinkle each tomato half with about 2 tablespoonfuls of the breadcrumb mixture. Broil 3 minutes or until topping is golden brown. Spoon sour cream on top of each tomato half. Makes 8 servings.

Herbed Swiss Potato Slices

Potato fans will love this robust side dish.

4 tablespoons butter or margarine
4 large baking potatoes, peeled,
    cut in 1/4-inch slices
Dried basil
Dried oregano
Salt

Freshly ground pepper
1/2 cup chopped onion
1/4 cup chopped green pepper
1/4 cup chopped pimiento
1 cup shredded Swiss cheese (4 oz.)
Snipped chives

In a large heavy skillet, melt butter or margarine. Place a single layer of potatoes in skillet. Sprinkle with basil, oregano, salt and pepper. Continue layering potatoes and seasonings until all potatoes are used. Cover and cook over medium heat 10 minutes. Turn potatoes by easing spatula under browned portion of potatoes on the bottom layer and turning carefully, a portion at a time. Add onion, green pepper and pimiento. Cover and cook 10 minutes longer or until potatoes are tender. Sprinkle with Swiss cheese. Cover and cook 1 to 2 minutes longer or until cheese melts. Sprinkle with snipped chives. Makes 4 to 6 servings.

Desserts

After a hearty brunch, serve a light dessert such as the Frosty Citrus Pie or Winter Fruit Compote. If you're looking for Minted Chocolate Mousse, it's on page 22. On the other hand, a light brunch needs to be followed by a substantial dessert. Devonshire Cheesecakes, page 14, have a seasonal fruit topping and a delicious rich cheese filling. The recipe for lovely fluted Cranberry Babas is on page 9.

Don't be afraid to make a dessert soufflé. They're really not as difficult as you may think. Make the Easy Apricot Soufflé the day before your brunch. It's the easiest of all.

Egg Whites are a basic ingredient of soufflés. Both sugar and cream of tartar help stabilize the foam of beaten egg whites. Add the sugar after the soft peaks have formed. This will cut down on the beating time. Then beat the egg whites to stiff—but not dry—peaks. When you lift the beaters, the peaks left on top of the beaten egg whites should stand straight; see photo on page 63. Overbeating breaks down the egg white foam and results in less volume and decreased stability.

Toasting Nuts brings out their flavor and they add a contrast in flavor and texture to a topping or sauce. To toast almonds or pecans, spread them on a baking sheet and put them in a 300°F (150°C) oven for several minutes, turning frequently to prevent scorching. Don't let them become too brown; they will darken as they cool. Let them cool before you attempt to use them.

Chocolate Curls are an effective dessert garnish and not difficult to make. Use a square or bar of chocolate that is soft enough to cut easily but not ready to melt. Shave off thin pieces with a vegetable peeler. You can pick up the curls with a wooden pick or skewer to place them on the dessert.

QUICK DESSERTS
- Use frozen pound cake as a base for shortcake. Top it with fresh or frozen fruits, frozen whipped topping, or ice cream sauce from the jar.
- Marinate fresh fruits in wine or spiced fruit juice. Serve them with very special crisp delicate cookies from your local gourmet shop.
- Stir sugar and chunks of appropriate fruit into fruit-flavored yogurt. Serve it in sherbet dishes or as a topping for cake squares.
- Top brownies from a mix with scoops of exotic coffee-based ice cream, then drizzle with coffee or chocolate liqueur or fudge topping.
- Set up a make-your-own-sundae bar. Use several kinds of ice cream, jam or prepared ice cream toppings, fruits, nuts and whipped cream.

Brandied Strawberries *Photo on page 5.*

Exquisitely flavored ice cream served with strawberries in ice-cold brandy snifters.

1 qt. vanilla ice cream	1 pint fresh strawberries, hulled, sliced
1/2 cup brandy	Orange-flavored liqueur

In a medium bowl, beat ice cream and brandy with electric mixer on low speed until slightly softened. Increase speed to medium and beat until smooth. Place mixture in freezer container. Cover and freeze 8 hours or overnight; mixture will not freeze solid. Chill 4 to 6 brandy snifters in the freezer. To serve, spoon ice cream mixture into chilled snifters. Top with strawberries and drizzle with orange-flavored liqueur. Makes 4 to 6 servings.

Strawberry Champagne Pie

An outstanding pie! Champagne adds a new flavor dimension.

1 envelope unflavored gelatin
1/3 cup sugar
1-1/4 cups pink champagne
1 pint strawberry ice cream, softened
1 (4-1/2-oz.) container frozen whipped
  topping, thawed (2 cups)

1 (9-inch) Basic Pastry shell, baked, page 57
Strawberry Glaze, see below
1-1/2 to 2 cups whole strawberries, hulled
Additional whipped topping, thawed
Fresh strawberries

Strawberry Glaze:
3/4 cup fresh strawberries, hulled
3/4 cup pink champagne
1/2 cup sugar

2 tablespoons cornstarch
Few drops red food coloring, if desired

In a medium saucepan, combine gelatin and sugar. Add champagne. Stir over medium heat until gelatin dissolves. Remove from heat. Add ice cream and stir until melted. Stir in 2 cups whipped topping. Beat with a whisk until smooth. Refrigerate until mixture mounds when dropped from a spoon, about 1 hour. Turn into pastry shell. Refrigerate until firm, 8 hours or overnight. Prepare Strawberry Glaze. Arrange whole strawberries on top of pie. Spoon cooled Strawberry Glaze over strawberries. Refrigerate until serving time. Cut into wedges to serve. Top wedges with additional whipped topping and strawberries. Makes 1 pie.

Strawberry Glaze:
In a saucepan, crush strawberries. Add champagne. Cook over medium heat 2 minutes. Put through a sieve. Combine sugar and cornstarch. Stir into strawberry mixture. Cook and stir until mixture is thickened and bubbly. Stir in red food coloring, if desired. Cool glaze at room temperature.

Peach-Berry Alaska Pie

The board is insulation so the pie shell won't overbake and the ice cream won't melt.

1 pint peach ice cream
1/4 cup flaked coconut
1/4 cup chopped pecans
1 (9-inch) Basic Pastry shell, baked, page 57
3 egg whites

1/2 teaspoon cream of tartar
1/2 teaspoon vanilla extract
1/3 cup sugar
3 cups sliced fresh peaches (about 4)
1 cup fresh or thawed frozen blueberries

In a medium bowl, let ice cream soften slightly at room temperature. Stir in coconut and pecans. Spread ice cream mixture in bottom of pastry shell. Freeze 8 hours or overnight until firm. Preheat oven to 475°F (245°C). In a small bowl, beat egg whites, cream of tartar and vanilla with electric mixer on high speed until soft peaks form. Gradually add sugar, beating until stiff peaks form. Remove pie from freezer. Top with peaches and blueberries. Top fruit with meringue, spreading and sealing to edge of pastry shell. Place the pie on a board. Bake pie on board 5 to 6 minutes or until meringue is lightly browned. Serve immediately. Makes 6 servings.

Frosty Citrus Pie

Serve this smooth, rich pie in small wedges.

4 tablespoons butter or margarine	3 egg yolks
1/2 cup brown sugar, firmly packed	1 cup whipping cream
1-1/2 cups wheat flakes cereal	1/2 teaspoon grated lemon peel
1/2 cup chopped pecans	3 tablespoons lemon juice
3 egg whites	1/2 teaspoon grated orange peel
1/2 cup granulated sugar	2 tablespoons orange juice

Butter a 9-inch pie plate; set aside. In a small saucepan, mix butter or margarine and brown sugar. Bring to a boil over medium heat, stirring occasionally. Simmer 1 minute. Stir in cereal and pecans. Spread on an ungreased baking sheet; cool. In a large bowl, beat egg whites with electric mixer on high speed until soft peaks form. Gradually add granulated sugar, beating until stiff peaks form; set aside. In a small bowl, beat egg yolks with electric mixer on high speed until thickened and lemon-colored, about 5 minutes. Fold egg yolks into egg white mixture. In a medium bowl, combine cream with lemon peel, lemon juice, orange peel and orange juice. Whip with electric mixer on high speed until soft peaks form. Fold whipped cream mixture into egg mixture. Crumble cooled cereal mixture. Sprinkle half the crumbled cereal mixture into the bottom of the buttered pie plate. Spoon whipped cream mixture on top of cereal mixture. Sprinkle with remaining cereal mixture. Freeze firm, 8 hours or overnight, but not over 2 days. Let stand at room temperature 15 minutes before serving. Makes one 9-inch pie.

Mocha Ribbon Pie

Next time you make this, try it with chocolate mint ice cream.

1 (5-1/3-oz.) can evaporated milk	1 qt. coffee ice cream, softened
1 (6-oz.) pkg. semisweet chocolate pieces	Whipped topping
1/2 (1-pint) jar marshmallow creme	Chocolate curls, page 141
4 tablespoons butter or margarine	
16 chocolate creme-filled cookies, crushed (1-1/2 cups)	

Butter a 9-inch pie plate; set aside. In a medium saucepan, mix evaporated milk and chocolate pieces. Stir constantly over low heat until chocolate melts. Beat in marshmallow creme with a wooden spoon. Refrigerate 2 hours or until cold. In a small saucepan, melt butter or margarine. Stir in cookie crumbs. Press crumb mixture into the buttered pie plate. Spread half the coffee ice cream in the pie shell. Top with half the cold chocolate mixture. Freeze 3 hours. Spoon the remaining ice cream on top of the pie. Top with remaining cold chocolate mixture. Freeze until firm, about 4 hours. Let stand at room temperature 15 minutes before serving. Garnish with whipped topping and chocolate curls. Makes one 9-inch pie.

Easy Apricot Soufflé

Prepared pudding and whipped topping make this as easy as it is good.

1 (3-oz.) pkg. apricot-flavored gelatin
2/3 cup apricot nectar
1 (17.5-oz.) can vanilla pudding
1 teaspoon grated lemon peel
2 tablespoons lemon juice

3 egg whites
1/4 cup sugar
1 cup whipped topping
Additional whipped topping
Fresh or canned whole apricots, quartered

Cut a strip of waxed paper to fit around a 1-quart soufflé dish. Coat one side of waxed paper with butter or margarine. Sprinkle with sugar. Place waxed paper, coated side in, around soufflé dish to form a collar extending about 1 inch above rim. If necessary, secure with a paper clip; set soufflé dish aside. In a medium saucepan, mix gelatin and apricot nectar. Stir constantly over medium heat until gelatin dissolves. Stir in pudding, lemon peel and lemon juice; mix until smooth. Refrigerate until partially set. In a large bowl, beat egg whites with electric mixer on high speed until soft peaks form. Gradually add sugar, beating until stiff peaks form. Fold apricot mixture into egg whites. Fold in 1 cup whipped topping. Spoon apricot mixture into the prepared soufflé dish. Refrigerate until firm, 6 hours or overnight. Carefully remove collar before serving. Garnish with additional whipped topping and apricot quarters. Makes 8 servings.

Harvey Wallbanger Soufflés

Refrigerated soufflés are served in wine glasses for a special occasion.

1/4 cup sugar
1 envelope unflavored gelatin
1-1/4 cups orange juice
3 egg yolks
2 tablespoons Galliano liqueur
2 tablespoons vodka

1 (4-1/2-oz.) container frozen
    whipped topping, thawed (2 cups)
3 egg whites
1/4 cup sugar
Additional whipped topping
Orange Twists, page 147

Butter six 8-ounce wine glasses. Sprinkle inside of each glass with sugar. Cut a strip of foil to fit around outside of each glass, extending about 1 inch above rim. Place foil collars around glasses. If necessary, secure with paper clips; set aside. In a medium saucepan, mix 1/4 cup sugar and gelatin. Add orange juice. Stir constantly over high heat until mixture boils and gelatin dissolves. Remove from heat. In a small bowl, beat egg yolks with electric mixer on high speed until thickened and lemon-colored, about 5 minutes. Stir 1/2 cup hot gelatin mixture into egg yolks. Add egg yolk mixture to gelatin mixture in saucepan. Stir constantly over medium heat until mixture thickens and coats a metal spoon. Remove from heat. Stir in Galliano and vodka. Refrigerate until partially set, stirring occasionally. Fold in 2 cups whipped topping. In a medium bowl, beat egg whites with electric mixer on high speed until soft peaks form. Gradually add 1/4 cup sugar, beating until stiff peaks form. Fold gelatin mixture into beaten egg whites. Spoon mixture into the prepared glasses. Cover and refrigerate until firm, 2 hours or overnight. Before serving, carefully remove collars. Garnish with additional whipped topping and orange twists. Makes 6 servings.

Grand Marnier Soufflés

You can omit the orange peel and substitute other flavored liqueurs.

4 tablespoons butter or margarine
1/3 cup all-purpose flour
3/4 cup milk
1/4 cup orange-flavored liqueur
1/3 cup granulated sugar

1/2 teaspoon grated orange peel
5 eggs, separated
2 tablespoons granulated sugar
1/2 teaspoon cream of tartar
Powdered sugar

Preheat oven to 350°F (175°C). Butter nine 6-ounce custard or soufflé cups. Sprinkle cups with sugar; set aside. In a small saucepan, melt butter or margarine. Blend in flour. Add milk, liqueur, 1/3 cup granulated sugar and orange peel. Stir constantly over medium-high heat until mixture thickens and bubbles. Remove from heat. In a large bowl, beat egg whites with electric mixer on high speed until soft peaks form. Add 2 tablespoons granulated sugar and cream of tartar. Beat until stiff peaks form. In a medium bowl, beat egg yolks with electric mixer on high speed until thickened and lemon-colored, about 5 minutes. Stir liqueur mixture into egg yolks. Slowly pour egg yolk mixture over egg whites, then gently fold together. Carefully pour 1/2 cup soufflé mixture into each prepared cup. Bake 25 to 30 minutes or until a knife inserted in center comes out clean. Sift powdered sugar over the top of the soufflé and serve immediately. Makes 9 servings.

How To Make Harvey Wallbanger Soufflés

1/Butter and sugar 6 wine glasses. Cut and fold strips of foil to fit around the rim of each glass and extend 1 inch above the rim. Fill glasses with soufflé mixture and refrigerate until firm.

2/To make Orange Twists, cut thin orange slices. Cut a slit in each slice just to the center. Twist the two cut edges in opposite directions and place an Orange Twist on top of each soufflé.

Splendid Chocolate Soufflé

This won't wait long after it's removed from the oven. Enjoy it immediately.

2/3 cup sugar
2 tablespoons cornstarch
1 cup milk
2 (1-oz.) squares unsweetened chocolate
4 eggs, separated

1/2 teaspoon salt
1/4 teaspoon cream of tartar
1 tablespoon butter or margarine, softened
1 teaspoon vanilla extract

Preheat oven to 350°F (175°C). Butter a 1-1/2-quart soufflé dish. Sprinkle dish with sugar; set aside. In a small heavy saucepan, blend 2/3 cup sugar and cornstarch. Gradually stir in milk. Add chocolate squares. Stir constantly over medium heat until chocolate melts and mixture thickens and bubbles. Remove from heat. In a medium bowl, beat egg whites with electric mixer on high speed until soft peaks form. Add salt and cream of tartar. Beat until stiff peaks form. In another medium bowl, beat egg yolks with electric mixer on high speed until thickened and lemon-colored, about 5 minutes. Gradually stir chocolate mixture, butter or margarine and vanilla into egg yolks. Slowly pour egg yolk mixture over egg whites, then gently fold together. Pour mixture into the prepared soufflé dish. Bake 50 minutes or until a knife inserted off-center comes out clean. Serve immediately. Makes 4 to 6 servings.

How To Make Strawberry Blintzes

1/Place about 1-1/2 tablespoons of yogurt mixture in the middle of each crepe. Fold the bottom edge of the crepe over the filling; fold each side over, then fold the remaining third of crepe over.

2/Brown the blintzes in butter or margarine, turning once. Be careful when you turn them so the filling doesn't leak out. Serve the blintzes topped with a sprinkling of powdered sugar and strawberry preserves.

Honeydew Ginger Boats

Look for candied or crystallized ginger in the supermarket gourmet section or in specialty shops.

1/4 cup chopped pecans
3 tablespoons butter or margarine
1 tablespoon cornstarch
2/3 cup whipping cream
1/3 cup light corn syrup

2 tablespoons finely chopped candied ginger
1/2 teaspoon vanilla extract
1 honeydew melon, cut in 8 wedges
1 qt. lime sherbet

Preheat oven to 300°F (150°C). Spread pecans on an ungreased baking sheet. Bake 15 minutes or until lightly toasted, stirring often; set aside. In a medium saucepan, melt butter or margarine. Blend in cornstarch. Add whipping cream, corn syrup and ginger. Stir constantly over medium-high heat until mixture thickens and bubbles. Simmer 1 minute. Stir in toasted pecans and vanilla. Cool. Place a melon wedge on each of 8 plates. Top each wedge with a scoop of sherbet. Drizzle each serving with about 2 tablespoons ginger sauce. Makes 8 servings.

Strawberry Blintzes

To save time on a busy morning, crepes can be made ahead, frozen in freezer bags and thawed.

1 cup all-purpose flour
3 tablespoons granulated sugar
1/4 teaspoon salt
3 eggs
1-1/3 cups milk
2 eggs

2 (8-oz.) cartons strawberry-flavored yogurt
1/2 cup strawberry preserves
Butter or margarine
Powdered sugar
Strawberry preserves

In a medium bowl, mix flour, granulated sugar and salt. In another medium bowl, mix 3 eggs and milk. Gradually add milk mixture to flour mixture, beating with electric mixer on medium speed until blended. Cover and chill for 2 to 3 hours. Prepare crepe pan according to manufacturer's directions or preheat a small shallow skillet. Brush with oil if pan does not have a non-stick finish. Using about 2 tablespoons batter for each crepe, cook on preheated crepe pan over medium-high heat until browned on bottom. To remove crepe, loosen edges and gently lift with a spatula. Stack crepes between squares of waxed paper for easy separation. In a medium bowl, slightly beat 2 eggs with a fork or whisk. Stir in yogurt and 1/2 cup strawberry preserves. Place crepes browned-side up and spoon about 1-1/2 tablespoons yogurt mixture onto the center of each crepe. Fold crepe over the filling: first the bottom, then the sides and finally the top, envelope-style. In a large skillet, melt 2 tablespoons butter or margarine. Brown blintzes over medium heat on both sides, adding more butter or margarine as necessary. Sprinkle blintzes with powdered sugar and top with a spoonful of strawberry preserves. Serve immediately. Makes 20 blintzes, about 10 servings.

Pralines & Cream Mold

A creamy mold topped with hot pecan sauce.

1 cup sugar
2 envelopes unflavored gelatin
4 cups half-and-half

2 teaspoons vanilla extract
Praline Sauce, see below

Praline Sauce:
1/2 cup butter or margarine
1 cup brown sugar, firmly packed
1/2 cup granulated sugar

1/4 cup bourbon
1/4 cup milk
1/2 cup toasted pecan halves, page 141

In a medium heavy saucepan, mix sugar and gelatin. Gradually stir in 2 cups half-and-half. Stir constantly over low heat until sugar and gelatin dissolve. Add remaining half-and-half and vanilla. Pour into a 1-quart mold. Refrigerate overnight or until firm. Before serving, prepare Praline Sauce. Unmold dessert onto a platter. Serve warm Praline Sauce separately. Makes 8 servings.

Praline Sauce:
In a small saucepan, melt butter or margarine. Stir in brown sugar, granulated sugar, bourbon, and milk. Stir constantly over medium heat until sugar dissolves. Stir in pecans. Makes 1-3/4 cups of sauce.

Spicy Baked Apples

You can substitute pears for apples and bake about 30 minutes.

6 large baking apples
1/2 cup golden raisins
1/4 cup chopped walnuts
1-1/2 cups brown sugar, firmly packed
1 cup cranberry-apple juice

3 tablespoons butter or margarine
1 teaspoon ground cinnamon
1/2 teaspoon ground nutmeg
Ice cream, if desired

Preheat oven to 375°F (190°C). Core apples. Peel a strip around the top of each apple. Place apples in a 10" x 6" baking dish. Fill apple centers with raisins and top with walnuts. In a small saucepan, mix brown sugar, cranberry-apple juice, butter or margarine, cinnamon and nutmeg. Bring to a boil over high heat, stirring occasionally. Pour syrup over apples. Bake 1 hour or until apples are tender, basting occasionally with syrup. Serve warm with ice cream, if desired. Makes 6 servings.

Zabaglione

Flavored with Marsala, an Italian wine, this custard can be served as a sauce or by itself.

4 egg whites
1/2 teaspoon cream of tartar
3 tablespoons sugar
4 egg yolks

3 tablespoons sugar
1/2 teaspoon vanilla extract
1/2 cup sweet Marsala
Assorted fresh fruits

In a medium bowl, beat egg whites and cream of tartar with electric mixer on high speed until soft peaks form. Gradually add 3 tablespoons sugar, beating until stiff peaks form; set aside. In the top of a double boiler, mix egg yolks, 3 tablespoons sugar and vanilla. Place over simmering water and beat with electric mixer on high speed until thickened and lemon-colored. Gradually add Marsala. Continue beating over simmering water until mixture mounds when dropped from a spoon, 10 to 12 minutes. Fold egg yolk mixture into beaten egg whites. Serve warm over fresh fruit in stemmed glasses. Makes 8 to 10 servings.

Peanutty-Granola Bars

These will tempt the "I don't want breakfast" crowd! Great for a dessert, too.

1 (14-oz.) pkg. chocolate caramels
2 tablespoons water
3/4 cup crunchy peanut butter

3 cups packaged plain granola
1 cup golden raisins
1/2 cup salted peanuts

Butter an 8-inch square dish; set aside. In a medium heavy saucepan, melt chocolate caramels and water over medium heat, stirring often. Stir in peanut butter until blended. Add granola, raisins and peanuts; mix well. Turn into the buttered dish; cool. Cut into 1" x 2" bars. Makes about 32 bars.

Winter Fruit Compote

Put this on the menu for your next holiday brunch.

2 pears, peeled, sliced
2 apples, peeled, sliced
1 cup cranberries
1 cup dried apricots
1/4 cup golden raisins

1 (22-oz.) can lemon pie filling
3/4 cup water
1/4 cup orange-flavored liqueur
1 teaspoon ground cinnamon
1/4 teaspoon ground nutmeg

Preheat oven to 350°F (175°C). In an 8-inch square baking dish, layer pears, apples, cranberries, apricots and raisins. In a medium bowl, mix pie filling, water, liqueur, cinnamon and nutmeg. Pour over fruits in the baking dish. Cover and bake 1 hour or until fruits are just tender. Let stand 45 minutes before serving. Stir gently and serve in dessert bowls. Makes 8 servings.

Krumkakes

Krumkake irons with cones are available in cookware shops and many department stores.

2 eggs
1/3 cup sugar
4 tablespoons butter or margarine, melted
1/2 teaspoon ground allspice
1/2 teaspoon orange extract

1/2 cup all-purpose flour
Vegetable oil
Whipped cream
Sliced fresh fruit
Grated orange peel

In a medium bowl, beat eggs with electric mixer on high speed until thickened, about 2 minutes. Gradually beat in sugar. Add butter or margarine, allspice and orange extract. Blend in flour by hand until smooth. Heat a seasoned 6-inch krumkake iron over medium heat until hot. When a drop of water sizzles on the iron, open the iron and brush lightly with oil. Spoon a heaping tablespoon of batter into center of iron. Close iron, scraping off any batter that leaks. Cook over medium heat 1 to 2 minutes on each side or until golden brown. Quickly shape the hot krumkake around the cone. Repeat with remaining batter. To serve, fill krumkake with whipped cream and fruit. Sprinkle with grated orange peel. Makes about 20 krumkakes.

How To Make Krumkakes

1/Using a krumkake iron, lower left, cook the batter on top of range. When cookies are browned on both sides, quickly roll them around the wooden accessory to make a cone.

2/Carefully fill the crisp cones with alternate spoonfuls of whipped cream and a mixture of fresh fruits.

Peachy-Almond Savarin

A savarin is a cake made with yeast batter, baked in a ring mold and soaked in syrup.

4-1/2 cups all-purpose flour
1/2 cup sugar
3 pkgs. active dry yeast
1 teaspoon salt
1-1/2 cups milk
3/4 cup butter or margarine

3 eggs
Almond Syrup, see below
Peach Glaze, see below
Crème Chantilly, see below
2 fresh peaches, peeled, sliced
Toasted whole almonds, page 141

Almond Syrup:
1 cup sugar
1 cup water
1/2 cup almond liqueur or peach brandy

Peach Glaze:
1 (12-oz.) jar peach preserves
1 tablespoon lemon juice

Crème Chantilly:
1 cup whipping cream (1/2 pint)
2 tablespoons powdered sugar
1/2 teaspoon vanilla extract

Generously grease a 12-cup fluted tube pan; set aside. In a large bowl, mix 1 cup flour, sugar, yeast and salt; set aside. In a small saucepan, mix milk and butter or margarine. Heat only until warm (120°F, 50°C); butter does not need to melt. Add milk mixture to flour mixture. Beat with electric mixer on medium speed 2 minutes, scraping bowl occasionally. Add eggs and 1/2 cup flour. Beat with electric mixer on high speed 2 minutes, scraping bowl occasionally. Stir in remaining 3 cups flour. Cover and let rise in a warm place about 1 hour or until doubled in bulk. Stir down batter and spoon into the greased tube pan. Cover and let rise in a warm place about 30 minutes or until doubled in bulk. Preheat oven to 350°F (175°C). Bake savarin 40 to 45 minutes or until nicely browned. While savarin is baking, prepare Almond Syrup, Peach Glaze and Crème Chantilly. Cool baked savarin in the pan 10 minutes. Invert to remove from pan. Place on rack over a shallow baking pan. Prick top of savarin all over with tines of a large fork. Drizzle with Almond Syrup a little at a time until all syrup is absorbed. Spoon Peach Glaze over savarin. To serve, fill center with Crème Chantilly. Garnish with peach slices and almonds. Makes 16 servings.

Almond Syrup:
In a small saucepan, mix sugar and water. Stir constantly over medium-high heat until sugar dissolves. Stir in liqueur or brandy. Cool.

Peach Glaze:
In a small saucepan, mix preserves and lemon juice. Stir constantly over medium heat until heated through. Put through a sieve.

Crème Chantilly:
In a medium bowl, beat whipping cream, powdered sugar and vanilla with electric mixer on high speed until soft peaks form.

Mom's Pound Cake

For a delicious shortcake base, omit the glaze.

6 eggs
2-1/2 cups sugar
1/2 cup shortening
1/2 cup butter or margarine, softened
2 teaspoons vanilla extract

4 cups all-purpose flour
2 tablespoons baking powder
1 teaspoon salt
2 cups milk
Glaze, see below

Glaze:
2 cups powdered sugar
1/4 cup milk or fruit juice

Preheat oven to 350°F (175°C). Generously grease a 10-inch tube pan; set aside. In a large bowl, mix eggs, sugar, shortening, butter or margarine and vanilla. Beat with electric mixer on high speed until fluffy. Stir together flour, baking powder and salt. Alternately add flour mixture and milk to creamed mixture, beating well with electric mixer on medium speed after each addition. Turn into the greased pan. Bake 60 to 70 minutes or until a wooden pick inserted in center comes out clean. Cool in pan 10 minutes. Invert to remove cake from pan and cool on rack. Prepare Glaze. Drizzle cake with glaze. Makes 16 to 20 servings.

Glaze:
In a medium bowl, mix powdered sugar and milk or juice. Beat until smooth.

Cherry-Berry Meringue Shortcakes

Vary the fresh fruit and fruit-flavored yogurt to suit the season.

2 egg whites
1/2 teaspoon vanilla extract
1/4 teaspoon cream of tartar
1/3 cup sugar
4 sponge cake dessert cups

1/2 cup fresh raspberries
1/2 cup pitted halved fresh dark cherries
1/2 cup lemon yogurt
1/4 cup whipped topping

Preheat oven to 450°F (230°C). Grease a baking sheet; set aside. In a medium bowl, beat egg whites, vanilla and cream of tartar with electric mixer on high speed until soft peaks form. Gradually add sugar, beating until stiff peaks form. Place sponge cake cups on the greased baking sheet. With a small spatula, spread meringue over cake cups, building up sides. Bake 5 to 6 minutes or until golden brown. Place on a rack to cool. Fill centers of cake cups with raspberries and cherries. In a small bowl, fold together yogurt and whipped topping. Spoon over fruit. Makes 4 servings.

Double-Chocolate Delight

Heavenly chocolate pudding-cake!

1 cup all-purpose flour
1/2 cup granulated sugar
3 tablespoons unsweetened cocoa powder
2 teaspoons baking powder
1/2 teaspoon salt
1/4 cup shortening
1/2 cup chopped walnuts

1/2 cup milk
1 teaspoon vanilla extract
1/2 cup brown sugar, firmly packed
1/2 cup light corn syrup
2 tablespoons cocoa powder
3/4 cup boiling water
Whipped cream or ice cream

Preheat oven to 350°F (175°C). In a medium bowl, thoroughly mix flour, granulated sugar, 3 tablespoons cocoa powder, baking powder and salt. Cut in shortening with a fork or pastry blender. Stir in walnuts, milk and vanilla; mix well. Spread batter in an ungreased 8-inch square baking dish. In a small bowl, mix brown sugar, corn syrup and 2 tablespoons cocoa powder. Add boiling water; mix well. Pour brown sugar mixture over batter in the baking dish. Bake 45 minutes, until a wooden pick inserted just halfway into cake comes out clean; pudding mixture on bottom of pan will be moist. Cool about 30 minutes before serving. Cut in small squares. Serve warm with whipped cream or ice cream. Makes 9 servings.

How To Make
Cherry-Berry Meringue Shortcakes

1/With a small spatula, spread meringue over sponge cake dessert cups, building up the sides to form a hollow big enough to hold a generous spoonful of fruit.

2/Bake the meringue cups until golden brown, then fill them with cherries and raspberries or your favorite fruit. Generously drizzle with the lemon-yogurt topping.

Strawberry Bavarian Cream

In a hurry? Use thawed frozen whipped topping in place of the whipping cream and sugar.

2 (10-oz.) pkgs. frozen strawberries in syrup,
   thawed
1 envelope unflavored gelatin
2 egg yolks

1-1/2 teaspoons vanilla extract
Few drops red food coloring, if desired
1 cup whipping cream (1/2 pint)
1/4 cup sugar

Drain strawberries, reserving 1 cup syrup in a small saucepan. Dissolve gelatin in syrup. Stir in strawberries and egg yolks. Stir constantly over medium heat until mixture thickens and coats a metal spoon. Stir in vanilla and food coloring, if desired. Refrigerate until mixture mounds when dropped from a spoon. In a medium bowl, beat cream and sugar with electric mixer on high speed until soft peaks form. Fold into strawberry mixture. Carefully spoon mixture into a 3-cup mold. Refrigerate until firm, about 3 hours or overnight. Makes 6 servings.

Variation

Raspberry Bavarian Cream: Substitute 2 (10-oz.) packages thawed frozen raspberries for the strawberries. Put raspberries through a sieve to remove seeds, if desired.

Pears Hélène

Ice cream and pears are topped with a glorious chocolate sauce.

1-1/2 cups water
1/2 cup sugar
1/4 cup dry sherry
1 tablespoon lemon juice

3 large pears, peeled, halved, cored
Chocolate Sauce, see below
Vanilla ice cream

Chocolate Sauce:
1 (14-oz.) can sweetened condensed milk
2 (1-oz.) squares unsweetened chocolate,
   broken in pieces

2 tablespoons reserved pear syrup
1 teaspoon vanilla extract

In a medium saucepan, mix water, sugar, sherry and lemon juice. Stir constantly over medium heat until sugar dissolves. Add pear halves. Bring to a boil over high heat. Reduce heat. Cover and simmer 10 to 12 minutes or until pears are tender, turning occasionally. Remove and reserve 2 tablespoons syrup to make Chocolate Sauce. Cool pears in remaining liquid. Prepare Chocolate Sauce. Place a large scoop of ice cream in each of 6 dessert bowls. Top with a pear half and drizzle with Chocolate Sauce. Makes 6 servings.

Chocolate Sauce:

In a small heavy saucepan, mix condensed milk, chocolate pieces, reserved 2 tablespoons pear syrup and vanilla. Stir constantly over low heat until chocolate melts. Cool at room temperature. Makes 3/4 cup of sauce.

Bananas Flambé

Glaze the bananas in a chafing dish or electric skillet at the table, then add the flaming rum.

1 (8-oz.) can pineapple chunks packed in juice
1/2 cup butter or margarine
1/2 cup brown sugar, firmly packed
1/2 cup chopped pecans
1/4 cup pineapple preserves

1/2 teaspoon ground cinnamon
4 bananas, peeled, cut in 1-inch pieces
1/4 cup rum or brandy
1 qt. butter pecan ice cream or
  vanilla ice cream

Drain pineapple, reserving 2 tablespoons juice. In a chafing dish or medium skillet, melt butter or margarine. Stir in pineapple chunks, reserved 2 tablespoons juice, brown sugar, pecans, preserves and cinnamon. Stir constantly over medium heat until brown sugar dissolves. Add bananas; reduce heat to low. Simmer uncovered 5 to 8 minutes or until tender, turning bananas occasionally to glaze. Heat rum or brandy in a small saucepan. Ignite and carefully pour flaming rum or brandy over bananas. When flame subsides, serve at once over ice cream. Makes 8 servings.

Grammy's Blueberry Pudding

Really a cake, this New England dessert is brimming with blueberries and topped with a lemon sauce.

1-1/2 cups fresh or well drained, thawed
  frozen blueberries
2 tablespoons all-purpose flour
1 egg
1/2 cup sugar
2 tablespoons butter or margarine, softened

1 teaspoon vanilla extract
1-1/2 cups all-purpose flour
2 teaspoons baking powder
1/4 teaspoon salt
1 cup warm milk
Lemon Hard Sauce, see below

Lemon Hard Sauce:
1/2 cup butter or margarine, softened
1 cup powdered sugar

2 tablespoons lemon juice

Preheat oven to 350°F (175°C). Grease a 6-cup ring mold; set aside. In a small bowl, toss blueberries with 2 tablespoons flour; set aside. In a medium bowl, beat egg, sugar, butter or margarine and vanilla with electric mixer on high speed until fluffy. Thoroughly stir together 1-1/2 cups flour, baking powder and salt. Alternately add flour mixture and warm milk to creamed mixture, beating well with electric mixer on medium speed after each addition. Fold in blueberries. Pour batter into the greased mold. Bake 30 to 35 minutes or until a wooden pick inserted in center comes out clean. While pudding is baking, prepare Lemon Hard Sauce. Cool pudding in mold 10 minutes. Remove from mold and cool slightly on rack. Serve warm with Lemon Hard Sauce. Makes 10 servings.

Lemon Hard Sauce:
In a small bowl, beat butter or margarine and powdered sugar with electric mixer on high speed until fluffy. Beat in lemon juice. Makes 1-1/2 cups of sauce.

Index

12.6795127329695